Philip Farkas

The Legacy of a Master

*The man who defined symphonic horn playing,
as seen through his writings and the
comments of colleagues and students.*

Edited and Collected
by M. Dee Stewart

The Instrumentalist Publishing Company

Table of Contents

Philip Farkas in Print

Notes to the Reader

Philip Farkas — it is safe to say that the name has great significance in the music world. Musical connoisseurs recognize Philip Farkas as a great horn artist through his concerts and recordings. Brass students know him as an outstanding teacher. His first book, *The Art of French Horn Playing* is studied in many instrumental methods classes. Performers regard Phil Farkas' career as the ultimate success story, and his name bears significant importance in the world of manufacturing with his development of the Farkas model horn for the Holton company. These outstanding contributions represent only a portion of the Farkas legacy, and through it all, Phil has remained approachable and amiable, kind and courteous, simply in love with life.

My involvement with Philip Farkas began as a student. His first book had just been published, a well-worn copy still in my studio with the price on the cover listed at $3.50. At that time his name represented just a book to me, but after hearing some performances of the Chicago Symphony, Farkas became a sound and standard for musicianship in my mind's ear. On one occasion I took my brother to hear the Chicago Symphony Woodwind Quintet where I summoned up the courage to meet this great man. From that day on Phil Farkas was a person to me; little did I know he would one day be a colleague and friend.

At Indiana University Phil has been a significant contributor to the success of the School of Music. He attained the prestigious rank of Distinguished Professor of Music and for twenty-four years produced students who continue to lend credibility to his pedagogy. Phil's experience and expertise, coupled with his insights and diligence, were productive in administrative as well as in human terms. In 1972 and again in 1980 he hosted the International Horn Workshop. The participants in 1980 numbered 520, one of the largest workshops ever organized for performers of a single instrument. From 1981 to 1984 Phil worked as a co-organizer of the Second International Brass Congress, a workshop for all brass instrumentalists with over 1300 in attendance.

In retirement, Phil and his wife Peggy enjoy a comfortable, relaxed life in Bloomington, Indiana, near their family and friends. Their home is close to the University and they are frequently seen at musical events and social functions. They remain an inspiration to all who know them.

M. Dee Stewart

M. Dee Stewart with Philip Farkas

M. Dee Stewart has been Professor of Trombone/Euphonium at Indiana University since 1980, following an eighteen year career with the Philadelphia Orchestra where he performed on tenor trombone, bass trombone, tenor tuba, and bass trumpet with the orchestra, made five recordings with the Grammy award-winning Philadelphia Brass Ensemble, and taught at the Curtis Institute of Music. He is active as a performer with orchestras and as a clinician and recitalist, and was one of the organizers of the Second International Brass Congress held at the Indiana University in 1984. In 1987 Arnold Jacobs: The Legacy of A Master; *edited and collected by Stewart, was published by the Instrumentalist Publishing Company.*

Comments by Philip Farkas

Being asked by Dee Stewart to be the subject of a book called *Philip Farkas, the Legacy of a Master* is quite overwhelming, and the fact that it follows a similar book celebrating the incomparable Arnold Jacobs makes the thought seem almost embarrassing. Dee is a very persuasive man who finally convinced me that there were enough people who had crossed my path over the last sixty years to make an interesting and informative book. Certainly these contributors who Dee has gathered together have done a lovely thing for me and I would like to thank them for their labor of love. Having so many friends is undoubtedly due to my being been in the music world for so long, rather than because of some endearing quality...of which I'm not aware. To have among these contributors friends, pupils, former pupils, performing colleagues, composers and conductors, is the most wonderful, exhilarating feeling I have experienced.

I am a little shy of that word, "Master," perhaps because none of us truly master our instrument, if we are objective about it. Perhaps it's because, when seeing my horn resting on a chair, I think, "There sits the master and here am I, the slave!" — albeit a loving one. I believe there is truth underlying this concept; the beginner is certainly the slave to the instrument, progressing over the years to the point where the slave and master finally form an inspired team, the listener enjoying the result of this happy marriage.

Helping others attain this happy marriage through teaching is, to me, the most satisfying objective of my life, superseding the intense pleasure of performing with a great orchestra. We all at times wonder, "What do I leave to posterity?" To me the most satisfying answer is, "I leave my students to posterity!" Being a link in the chain extending from music's past to music's future is the most fulfilling aspect of my life.

To Dee Stewart I give my gratitude for conceiving this book and bringing it all together into a cohesive, attractive form. It takes musical expertise, fine writing ability, artistic judgment and a love for hard work to compile a book such as this. All of these qualities are found in Dee Stewart; Dee is the real master behind this book!

Philip Farkas

Chapter One

My Life in Music

Phil Farkas, age 19 1st Horn, Kansas City Philharmonic

My Beginnings

My mother spent her early childhood in the St. Vincent Orphanage in Chicago and was later adopted by the Harry Cassady family, well-to-do people who lived in a large home on Chicago's south side. As a young woman, she became a professional photographer and worked Automobile Row on south Michigan Avenue, photographing the latest model cars by using the cumbersome wet plate cameras of the time. I remember having the thrill not so long ago of seeing a display of historic automobile photographs and among them were several signed "Anna Cassady."

The son of Hungarian immigrants, my father was accepted at Purdue. His family, consisting of old-fashioned Europeans, insisted that he pursue a degree in civil engineering. He did so to please them, although engineering held little interest for him; his real love was writing. He was able to support himself through his college years by selling a couple of short stories a month to *Adventure Magazine* for $50 each. In the early 1900s, $50 was a lot of money. From time to time he would boast, the way fathers do, about playing football in college. Naturally, I took it all with a grain of salt. The Chicago Symphony played several concerts on the Purdue campus and on one of these occasions I wandered over to the gym where they had pictures of every football team since the first one, and there on the 1904 squad was Emil Farkas. After his graduation he teamed up with his younger brother, who had studied art in Paris, and began an advertising agency that still exists today.

My parents had no formal musical training, nevertheless my father could whistle a recognizable "Yankee Doodle" and my mother could sing in a beautiful, clear soprano voice with exceptionally fine intonation. At the time of my birth in 1914 we lived in Elmhurst, a suburb of Chicago. Both my mother and I were afflicted with asthma and the family moved around the country, trying to find a place where we wouldn't have an allergic reaction. At age six I lived in California for a few months; at age seven I moved to Arizona. Nothing helped so we returned to Chicago, and because of all this moving I didn't start first grade until I was eight years old.

Eventually, the Farkas family settled on the south side of Chicago in a neighborhood called Avalon Park, and I attended the local elementary school there. Because I started so late I was two years older than all the other kids, but things evened out a little when I skipped second grade.

It was at Emil G. Hirsch Junior High School that I began my musical studies. Because I didn't get along with the gym teacher, my parents and the school principal felt I could best fulfill my physcal education requirements by joining the marching band.

The tuba appealed to me, and for several months I worked with an old BB♭ Pan American, becoming so proficient that I was invited to play "My Old Kentucky Home" at a school assembly. However, my tuba playing didn't last long, after the streetcar conductor refused to have an instrument that size inconveniencing the other passengers. I immediately went to Lyon and Healy's and rented something considerably smaller, a French horn.

Once in high school, I quickly learned that playing horn was what I wanted to do with my life. Despite the lack of a formal musical education in my parents' background, they encouraged me towards my professional goal with loving enthusiasm. No matter how minimal my participation in a school musical activity might have been, both my parents were always in attendance. Despite the financial hardships caused by the Depression, my father bought me my first double horn in 1930; that was a year when his advertising business was completely dormant. He also helped me pay for horn lessons with the great Louis Dufrasne. I paid for them with the money I made ushering evenings at Orchestra Hall; not only did I make $1.25 per night, but I was able to hear the Chicago Symphony several times a week.

Somehow I found time during those high school years to attend rehearsals of the Chicago Civic Orchestra, which was and still is the training school of the Chicago Symphony Orchestra. After three years I won the first horn position with the newly formed Kansas City Philharmonic and left Chicago without graduating from high school. Years later, when I was in the Chicago Symphony, this bothered me so much that I attended night school, made up the few missing credits, and finally earned my high school diploma.

Krueger and Kansas City

When I played with the Kansas City Philharmonic from 1933 to 1936, the first permanent conductor I worked under was Karl Krueger. At the time I was only 18 years old, but I had three years of experience playing in the Chicago Civic Orchestra. Krueger may not have been a great conductor, but he was certainly an adequate one. The one thing that distinguished him was that he was a very polished speaker and an erudite man. One time when we were performing in Winfield, Kansas, he asked us if we would like to see him arrange an engagement for the orchestra for the following year. During intermission he went on stage and made a brief speech in which he told the audience, "You consider yourselves to

Karl Krueger

4

be out in the prairie lands of the Midwest, but you are the center — not only of the population and perhaps the geographical center, but the center of culture in this country as well." He went on in that vein for quite some time, stressing how the Midwest is the true cultural center of this country. After we finished the concert, a committee from the town of Winfield came backstage and, as Krueger predicted, engaged the orchestra for the following year.

Once when the Kansas City Orchestra was returning home on a long sleeper train, one of the guys suggested we go in the baggage car to play poker. We went back to our sleeping compartments, changed into our pajamas so we'd be comfortable, and headed toward the game.

There were six of us, sitting on trumpet cases or whatever we could find, using the tympani trunk as our card table. The game was so engrossing that none of us noticed what time it was. Finally we realized that the train hadn't moved for a long time and threw open the side doors of the car. The sun was just coming up, the rest of the train nowhere in sight. We later found out that the train had violated railroad regulations because of its length and therefore dropped the baggage car off on a siding. Pretty soon another train came along, picked us up, and took us into the station in Kansas City. The six of us in pajamas had to walk through the long and crowded depot. Luckily we had plenty of money from the poker game so we could afford a cab to take us to our apartments.

Frederick Stock, Chicago 1936

Three years later there was a first horn opening in Chicago when Pellegrino Lecce returned to Italy because his mother was dying. He was only in his thirties, so it was unexpected that this opening would occur. I found out later that the Chicago Symphony used the Kansas City Philharmonic the way a major league ball club uses the minor leagues; they had farmed me out to Kansas City to get some experience before playing in Chicago. Even though I had played an audition for Kansas City, people from the Chicago Symphony had already asked Krueger to take me. At 21 I signed my Chicago Symphony contract, although I didn't actually play my first note as the principal horn until I was 22.

Frederick Stock was my new boss when I joined the Chicago Symphony in 1936. I think he was underestimated and underrated as a conductor; as I look back, I realize that he was one of the finest, smartest conductors I have ever worked with, although at the time I had no way of comparing him because I had so little experience at that point in my life. Stock loved program variety, and we played five or six concerts a week, all different and well done, as some of the old recordings will show.

The symphony season then consisted of 28 winter weeks, 6 weeks of concerts at Ravinia, and summer concerts in Grant Park. We had two weeks of those at the same time we had Ravinia: Monday and Wednesday were at Grant Park and Tuesday, Thursday, Saturday, and Sunday were at Ravinia. My first week with the Chicago Symphony started in June, and we played six different concerts in five days. I stayed in Chicago for five years, starting with the 1936-37 season and ending with the 1940-41 season, the 50th anniversary of the orchestra. Once a week that year we premiered a new work, one of which was Stravinsky's Symphony in C.

Stock liked to shorten the Friday afternoon concerts a little so the ladies in the audience could catch their train. His idea was to use silent gestures to communicate his desires to the orchestra. Prior to this he often whispered his instructions for second endings or cuts to the first cellist, who then relayed it to the person next to him and so on until it had been passed through the entire orchestra.

He hit upon the idea of using hand signals as was done in radio. After several trips to local stations, he instructed us in this newly acquired art. "When I hold up one finger, that means take the second ending. When I hold up two fingers, that means take the first ending." His thinking was that if he held up one finger, he only wanted us to go through the passage once. This kind of logic was pretty confusing to us; worse still, he had a number of other hand signals, too.

One day for a pops concert we were going to play *Voices of Spring* which begins with two horns holding notes a fifth apart. Stock often eliminated the long introduction of this piece when playing it for an encore; instead, he'd start with Waltz No. 1. At this time he held up his first finger and Max Pottag, who was then second horn, and I put our horns down because we had eight bars rest at the Waltz. Stock gave a downbeat; absolute silence ensued. He gave us a dirty look and turned to the audience. "Ladies and gentlemen," he announced in his thick German accent, "you have just witnessed the finest pianissimo ever achieved in Orchestra Hall."

Stock decided to record the Brahms 3rd Symphony in Lieder-kranz Hall while the orchestra was on tour in New York. Lie-derkranz was a famous old hall with excellent acoustics, and Stock never quite liked the sound of recordings made in Chicago. We played the Brahms on an evening concert in Carnegie Hall and were set to record it the next morning at 9:00. After the evening performance it occurred to me that my lip would stay in better shape if I just stayed up all night, that way I wouldn't have to get up early in the morning and warm up all over again. This was the

Frederick Stock

7

first time I had been in New York, so a bunch of us went to Lindy's for cheesecake and stayed out all night. I returned to my room around seven in the morning, shaved and showered and went down to the hall to get ready for the recording session. As I walked backstage, I saw the orchestra's principal clarinetist passed out on a bass trunk. Everybody was upset because the Brahms 3rd is practically a clarinet concerto, but it was of no use, we couldn't revive him. He had the same idea I did but evidently overdid it.

I look back on those years now and realize that Stock had the biggest repertoire of any conductor I ever worked with. He conducted works of composers whose names were not even known. Stock's loyalty sometimes prevented the orchestra from becoming what it could be; he had wonderful woodwind players, but a few of the brass might have been past their time. I remember when we played the Beethoven 5th at the dedication of the newly refurbished Auditorium. The assistant horn, an older man beyond his prime, played during one of the grand pauses. Stock called me in his room after the concert and said, "We must get rid of that nitwit, we've got to fire him," but then he reflected for a while and said, "No, we can't do that because nobody else will hire him. He must be kept."

Stock was very kind to me. I was only 21 and very inexperienced when I got that job. He would often call me into his office and tell me how he wanted certain passages played so he wouldn't embarrass me at the rehearsal.

Stock had studied composition and conducting with Richard Strauss, who had told Stock exactly how he wanted the *Till Eulenspiegel* horn call played. In one of our meetings, Stock related these instructions to me in his office. After Stock died we had the famous Viennese musician, Karl Böhm, as guest conductor and we played *Till*. When I opened my music before the second concert, there was an autographed picture of Böhm. Afterwards I thanked him and asked what the occasion was for this gift. "In all my touring of the United States," he said, "you are the only horn player to play the *Till Eulenspiegel* call correctly." "There's a reason for that, sir," I told him, "Richard Strauss told Frederick Stock how to do it, and Frederick Stock told me."

Bohm laughed at this. "No wonder you did it right. I was in the same class that day with Stock when Strauss told us about the horn call."

Love and Marriage

I have the philosophy that people should love life because no one knows what's around the corner. My life has often changed direction by pure coincidence, such as the time the streetcar conductor wouldn't allow me to bring my tuba on board.

One other coincidence occurred when I was 25 and dating a student at the Chicago Musical College, where I taught. She was about my age, being an older student while I was a very young teacher. She had the annoying habit of not being ready on time; I'd often make a reservation at a nice restaurant and wind up losing it because she wasn't ready when I'd pick her up.

On one occasion I had a date to meet her at the college. The time came and she was nowhere to be seen. I was about to lose another reservation when I saw Peggy Groves, a voice student and good friend of the girl I was dating. Out of exasperation I said, "Hey Peggy, do you want to go to dinner?" Her answer was an enthusiastic, "Yes!"

As we got off the elevator I saw my date entering the building. It was an uncomfortable moment, but I haven't had any dates with her since. Peggy and I hit it off so well that we dated regularly and two years later we were married.

During this time I was the youngest principal player in the Chicago Symphony and also the lowest paid. My former job as an usher at Orchestra Hall came back to haunt me because despite the fact that I was the orchestra's principal horn, the manager still thought of me as a kid handing out programs. Whenever I asked for a raise he would remind me that just a few years earlier I was making $1.25 a night. I finally gave up on ever getting a suitable raise in Chicago. After five years with Stock, I had an opportunity to go to the Cleveland Orchestra which paid better while being equally prestigious.

In those days there were no auditions, and Artur Rodzinski had been a guest conductor at Ravinia, liked the way I played, and gave me the principal horn position in Cleveland. Peggy was pregnant when I accepted Rodzinski's generous offer, and by the time we left Chicago our baby was five weeks old. I drove the car with a trailer full of furniture, while Peggy and the baby flew.

Artur Rodzinski, Cleveland 1941

My new boss Rodzinski was an intense man, certainly a type-A person. He took all his tempos rather fast and liked to rehearse at lightning speed. When he announced a rehearsal letter he'd give you about one second to find it on the page before the downbeat. He was not a kindly man and was demanding, expecting the best at all times.

For one program Rodzinski resurrected a number by Franz Liszt called "St. Francis Talking to the Birds." The birds were the flutes and St. Francis was the horn. It started out with 24 measures of solo horn; it was enough to make me nervous. Just as I was nearing the end and thinking, "Thank God only two more notes," someone in the audience started coughing. Rodzinski stopped, pulled out his handkerchief and waved it at the person in the audience, then started the whole thing over again.

The night before we recorded the Mendelssohn *Midsummer Night's Dream* in 1941, Rodzinski called me at home and told me to use vibrato on the recording. I had never done this and wondered how I could master vibrato in less than 12 hours. I called the orchestra's third horn who had experience with this and he told me to wiggle the fingertips of my right hand inside the bell, which would act like the little rotors inside a vibraphone.

As we were about to start, Rodzinski announced that everything would be done in one take so no one was to make a mistake. If this weren't upsetting enough, he then called me aside and told me to play the climactic B near the end an octave higher.

Towards the conclusion of the recording I began to feel like a baseball pitcher with a no-hitter going; everything was working fine but one broken note would ruin everything. I recorded it with the high B included and it seemed to me from that day on everybody had to do it that way. Nothing was ever said to me about it in Chicago but I always did it, because if I didn't, everybody might think I was slipping. Musically it is logical but Mendelssohn probably realized that it was too risky for the horn players of his time. The recording originally came out on 78 but was later reissued on the Columbia Entre Series. Whenever I listen to it I am thankful that I don't hear any vibrato in my sound.

One of the most unusual memories I have of Rodzinski is a Cleveland Orchestra tour during World War II. Rodzinski commissioned Robert Russell Bennett to arrange a bunch of tunes from Jerome Kern's *Showboat* into a lengthy concert piece. We not only recorded it, but we took it out and played it every night on the road; it got to the point that we actually knew it from memory.

We stopped in Winston-Salem, North Carolina to play at an all-girl's school. Because of the war there were intermittent blackouts that came without warning, even the lights in public halls and auditoriums were turned out. As we were about to begin the concert, the auditorium went completely black; nothing was visible. All of a sudden we heard Rodzinski ask for a cigarette lighter. "*Showboat*," he announced to the orchestra as he lit a cigarette. All we could see to follow was the glowing tip of his cigarette; we played the whole thing in the dark and brought the house down.

Leinsdorf in Cleveland

Rodzinski left Cleveland for the New York Philharmonic and was eventually replaced by Erich Leinsdorf. Unfortunately, this was during WWII and in 1944 Leinsdorf was drafted. Louis Davidson, the principal trumpet player, and I were very close to him; Leinsdorf would often drop by Davidson's house in the evenings and the three of us would drink beer together. When it was time for him to go into the Army we insisted on driving him to the train.

We picked him up at six in the morning. He wore a derby hat and beautifully fitted overcoat with a velvet collar, under his arm a copy of Kant's *Critique of Pure Reason*. We took him to the station where he joined a group of enlistees. The sergeant yelled, "Form a column of twos and follow me." The last I saw of him was a back view with his derby hat, velvet-collared overcoat, and volume of Kant under his arm, marching alongside a guy in torn clothes and a leather jacket.

A few months later he was discharged.

November 23, 1979

Dear Dean Webb,

    Mr. Leinsdorf would like to thank you for your letter to him of November 2nd, regarding Mr. Philip Farkas.

    As Mr. Leinsdorf is presently out of town, he asked that I write this letter of his highest praise for Mr. Farkas. He holds Mr. Farkas in great esteem as a musician and is quite happy to recommend him for the distinguished appointment you are considering. With best regards.

Sincerely,
Nancy Dodds
for Erich Leinsdorf

Erich Leinsdorf

Odd Jobs

Cleveland didn't have a summer season so I returned to Chicago and picked up what work I could. One summer I subbed for Frank Brouk at N.B.C. and played a program called *The Farm and Home Hour*, which started at eight in the morning and was broadcast all over the country. The union wouldn't let us play before eight so we would start the broadcast without any rehearsal.

One morning as we were waiting to see what the first number would be, in walked the principal cellist, Ennio Bolognini. He was

12

a big, dashing guy who loved to wear uniforms; all his clothes had wings or some military insignia on them. Regardless of the fact that he had never been in the service, he always bought his clothes at an army surplus store. The guy was a womanizer, gambler, race car driver, stunt pilot, and for a time played principal cello in the Chicago Symphony. He was fired, not for musical reasons, but for being unreliable; Errol Flynn had nothing on Ennio.

On this particular morning he brought with him a beautiful Great Dane dog. Ennio had been at an all-night poker game and the host had lost everything and put the dog down to cover his last bet. Ennio was clearly the winner and not having time to deposit his winnings at his apartment, brought the dog straight from the poker game to the 8:00 a.m. broadcast.

A minute or two before airtime, the conductor announced that we would be starting with Massanet's *Elegy* for cello and orchestra, the solo to be played by Bolognini. Ennio took out his cello and secured the dog by sliding the loop at the end of the leash under one of the chair legs.

Unfortunately, the dog had only known Ennio for an hour or so. When he began the *Elegy*, the poor animal became terrified and began backing up, pulling Ennio, the chair, and cello with him across the highly polished linoleum floor. Unbothered by such a minor inconvenience, Ennio rested the back of his cello on his knees and continued playing.

The announcer, realizing the distance between the soloist and microphone was increasing, grabbed a mike stand and began in hot pursuit. In addition to being frightened by the sound of the cello, the animal was now being chased by a man holding a large stick-like object. The Great Dane accelerated his retreat, still pulling a performance of Massenet behind him.

Although he didn't miss a single note, we calculated that Ennio traveled at least 200 feet during the first few minutes of that broadcast. Too bad it wasn't on television.

Koussevitzky and Boston

After four years in Cleveland I left for the Boston Symphony to play alternate first horn with Willem Valkenier. I had my own quartet and Willem had his. There were nine horns in the Boston Symphony then and poor Osbourne McConathy played assistant to both Willem and me.

13

Serge Koussevitzky, my new boss, was an exciting conductor; his face would get red and the veins in his forehead would stick out in intense passages. All of us thought that if we made a mistake during one of these passages, he'd probably drop dead and it would be our fault.

Koussevitzky murdered the English language, and it was fun to listen to him when he was angry. One time when a bassoon player couldn't get the right note, he said, "All right, play it vat you vant."

Serge Koussevitzky

He often said, "You play like a bunch of government employers." He was another demanding conductor; it seems that all my bosses were that way. When I had a heart attack in 1978, the doctors inquired what might have caused it because I was in good health and did everything right. "Were you ever subjected to stress?" they finally asked me.

"Stress!" I said. "My God, I was the principal horn under Rodzinski, Koussevitzky, Szell, and Reiner!"

That seemed to be the answer.

Koussevitzky was not the schooled musician that George Szell was. He was a virtuoso bass player and played with great expression. As a conductor he took occasional liberties with the music, but he gave the audience exciting and often inspired concerts. He was quite a contrast to Artur Rodzinski.

During my year at Boston the orchestra played in New York several times. On one of those trips I got a call at my hotel from Artur Rodzinski, who told me to meet him at seven the next morning in the Carnegie Pharmacy.

I walked into the drugstore at the appointed hour and saw no one except a huddled-up man at the end of the counter. I couldn't see who it was because he had his hat pulled down over his head and his overcoat collar turned up. I moved close enough to him to see that it was Rodzinski. He signaled me to sit down and began talking in hushed tones about my coming to the New York Philharmonic where he was now the music director. "Phil," he said, "I want you in the Philharmonic." I was flattered, but luckily didn't pursue it; Rodzinski had a falling out with the management and was fired as music director.

Szell in Cleveland

After one year of playing with both Koussevitzky and the Boston Symphony and Fiedler and the Boston Pops, George Szell invited me to return to Cleveland, where he was now the new director. Szell was a known quantity to me, having been a guest conductor on many occasions. I couldn't resist his invitation because I thought of him as one of the great conductors of all times.

He was a precise musician, at times he even conducted cadenzas. The orchestra always sounded fluent and often spontaneous, but I guarantee you that spontaneity was well rehearsed.

George Szell

December 3, 1969

Dear Phil,

Thank you very much for your letter of November 22nd. It reached me just on the day we had auditions for fourth horn and we engaged a New York player who had already played very often and for prolonged periods with the Philharmonic as substitute. He played a very satisfactory audition, both in solo and horn quartet playing.

I hope all is well. Whenever I hear from you, that summer comes back to mind when I did the Brahms cycle at Ravinia in which you played all soli unforgettably.

Cordially,

George Szell

I had a couple years with Szell, who was probably the best schooled musician I played under. He knew his theory, was a tremendous pianist, knew how to conduct, and was good at explaining why and how he wanted certain effects from the orchestra. Once when we were doing the *Sinfonietta* by Janacek, the viola player told him there was a passage that simply could not be played. Szell instructed them to put their thumb down on the fingerboard as a cellist does and finger above the thumb, fretting the fingerboard.

As a student horn player in Czechoslovakia, he knew the instrument so well that on several occasions he actually told me what fingering to use on the horn, although sometimes his suggestions weren't that comfortable.

Szell maintained that Beethoven wrote the greatest nine symphonies and the sixth was the best. One particular time we had just finished rehearsing it and were scheduled to play it that night. As I walked off the stage, Szell informed me that he wanted the opening of the finale played on the natural F horn. It is possible but very difficult, and because the rehearsal was over, I wouldn't get a chance to try it. I went home and attempted to take my usual afternoon nap before the concert, but it was useless. Finally, I hit upon a solution: before the horn solo begins, there is a 36-bar rest, and every time Szell looked in another direction I raised my music stand an inch or so. By the time we got to the solo the only parts of me he could see were my eyes and the bridge of my nose. I used the usual fingering and the solo went well. When I came off the stage he caught me and said, "You see, it is so much better that way." We took it on tour that year and I did the same thing several more times. These things happen from time to time. It's important to please the conductor but at the same time you have to protect yourself as well.

Rodzinski in Chicago

After working with Szell I was invited back to Chicago by Artur Rodzinski, who arrived there by way of Cleveland and New York. I accepted for several reasons: I admired Rodzinski greatly, enough years had passed so the Chicago Symphony management no longer thought of me as a $1.25-a-night usher, and Chicago was home to me. Unfortunately, in Rodzinski's 15th week he was given his notice, but his contract allowed him to finish 15 more weeks.

There were several things that led to his dismissal: one of them had to do with the time the Chicago Symphony played a concert in Green Bay, Wisconsin. The Green Bay people insisted a clause be put in the contract requiring Rodzinski's presence for the performance because he was well known for not showing up. Before the concert the stage manager came out and told the audience that Artur Rodzinski could not be there that night because he had bursitis. "He cannot even lift his arms above his waist," were the stage manager's words. The audience booed and hissed. Our assistant conductor, Tauno Hannikainen, came out and we played a good concert for him.

Artur Rodzinski

18

The incident would have been forgotten, but unfortunately for Rodzinski, the Chicago *Tribune* hit the streets the next day with a society feature called "They Were There," which consisted of photographs of prominent Chicagoans at various social functions. In the center of the page was a picture of Rodzinski raising a glass of champagne over his head. The worst part of it was that the newspaper clipping said the party took place at the same time the concert was being played in Green Bay; people in Green Bay also got the Chicago *Tribune*.

Another time he gave a party and invited the Ryersons of Ryerson Steel and the Swifts of the meatpacking family; both Edward Ryerson and Charles Swift were on the board of directors of the Symphony. These important guests stayed in the living room, but Rodzinski invited several of the orchestra players to go into his bedroom to say hello to him. "Come in, boys, and we'll talk," he said while laying on a lounge in his pajamas.

The conversation was mostly about music, but soon Mrs. Rodzinski came in. "Artur," she said, "the guests are getting impatient."

"Tell them to go to hell," he said, and continued talking with us. She came back two or three times and said the same thing. He kept telling her to tell them to go to hell.

She came back one last time and said, "Artur, the guests are going home."

"Good," he said, and continued talking to us.

Rodzinski asked me to drive him home after concerts because it was on my way. On one of these trips he disclosed his plans to move the Chicago Symphony from Orchestra Hall to the Auditorium. He liked this building because it was bigger than Orchestra Hall, and we would be able to put on an occasional opera. I told him that the idea was a mistake and that people who have box seats at Orchestra Hall have had them for years and bequeathed them to their heirs in their wills; those people would never leave Orchestra Hall.

Unfortunately he did not take my advice and when he informed the public of his plans to move the orchestra, there was a terrific outcry. Coupled with the Green Bay debacle and the way he treated the important people on the board of directors, it led to his dismissal.

His was an exciting downfall. At concerts towards the end of the season, somebody would always jump up and yell, "Fire the manager, not the conductor!" Somebody else would tell that person to shut up; fist fights frequently erupted. At the last few concerts, policemen were stationed at the end of every aisle to maintain order. On his final concert Rodzinski conducted "The Stars and Stripes Forever" and they let down a huge American flag as the number progressed. He returned for his final bows with his little boy, Ricky, in his arms. The audiences loved him; the management couldn't stand him.

Rafael Kubelik

After Rodzinski left Chicago we had a season of guest conduc-

Rafael Kubelik

20

tors, and then Raphael Kubelik was appointed permanent conductor. His father was a great violinist, and Kubelik knew everything about strings but nothing about winds. Consequently, he was happiest when we were subdued, and he usually left us alone.

Once he called the second horn, Clyde Wedgwood, and me aside just before the orchestra was to make a weekly television appearance. "I got a postcard today that said in last week's broadcast you were taking the water out of your horns when the camera was on you. The person who wrote the postcard thought it was quite disgusting to see you dumping the water out of your horn, so don't do that," he instructed.

"You mean we're not supposed to take the water out of our horns?" I asked.

"You heard me. Do not take the water out of your horns!"

We smiled, and because there was nothing important on the program except for a lot of loud playing, we simply kept the water in for an hour. By the end of the program everything we did had a gurgled sound. We tried to be discreet about it so we wouldn't spoil anything, but Kubelik could hear it. As soon as it was over he rushed back and yelled, "Are you trying to make fun of me? What are you doing with that funny sound?"

I said, "We're not trying to make fun of you, you told us not to take the water out of our horns and that's what we did."

"What difference does that make?" he snarled.

I was mad as hell; I took the slide out of my horn and dumped a teacup of water on his shoe. "That's the difference," I told him.

W.G.N. Radio

In addition to keeping up with the symphony schedule I did some work for W.G.N. radio. One time they asked me to play first horn because their regular first horn was sick. I was to play the overture to *Martha*, which has a beautiful, long horn solo. I have to admit I was pretty nervous; the orchestra was strange to me, and they played a little lower in pitch than we did in the symphony. I noticed they were all taking little sly looks at me. The fact that no one in the orchestra took anything seriously worried me even more.

In addition to being nervous, I wasn't prepared for the way I started to sweat. "This thing can't be this hard," I thought. When it was over, I was sweating profusely. As I stood up I noticed a flickering light; somebody had stuck a lighted candle under my cane-bottomed chair.

Another time Michael Wilkomirski, the concertmaster, had to play the famous Hungarian violin solo, *Gypsy Airs*. At the rehearsal the man in the sound booth told him to finish the slow solo introduction section from his usual seat, then walk over to the microphone to play the fast spiccato part because the sound wouldn't be picked up otherwise.

Wilkomirski, a short, stocky fellow who was completely bald, was a terrific fiddle player. Anyway, one of the other guys got an idea. He went to a Western Tire and Auto Store and bought a suction cup with three little American flags sticking out of it; in those days people used to put them on their dashboards during patriotic holidays.

The night of the broadcast the concertmaster finished the big schmaltzy solo and began to leave his chair for the microphone. The guy behind him stood up and stuck the suction cup right on top of his bald head. Wilkomirski didn't have time to remove it; he had a fiddle in one hand and a bow in the other and had to get to the microphone before the spiccato section began. He wound up playing the rest of the solo with three American flags sticking out of his head while the studio audience looked on.

There was another audience show at W.G.N. where we had to wear little red bolero jackets that looked like something a waiter would wear, except they had two buttons in the back like a suit coat. Once again Wilkomirski was the fall guy; one of the musicians sitting behind him took thread off an oboe reed and wound it around Wilkomirski's two back buttons and the rung of his chair. When he stood to play his solo at the microphone, he couldn't get up. Finally, through superhuman effort he made it over to the mike with the chair hanging from his backside, swinging to and fro as he played the solo.

Other Interests

From 1947 to 1960 my family lived in Evanston, the suburb immediately north of Chicago. During those years the orchestra played a ten-concert series in Milwaukee, and those of us who lived north could be home in bed a couple hours sooner than the south siders. Living there was also an advantage during the summer season when the orchestra was at Ravinia, which was quite a ways north of the city.

Our house was a magnificent old home, one the realtors considered a white elephant. It had 21 rooms, 6 fireplaces, a 3rd floor ballroom complete with bandstand and a two-story ceiling replete with brass chandeliers. The place was inexpensive to purchase; don't ask about the upkeep.

It was during our Evanston years that I was asked by the Frank Holton Company to design a new double horn for them. The project came about in a peculiar way: in 1956 I was invited to dinner by Traugott Rohner, the publisher of *The Instrumentalist*, because I was going to write an article for the magazine. Also invited were several executives from the Holton Company, who were there to discuss advertising. They introduced themselves as Elliot Kehl and Theodore Kexel. As we sat around talking, one of them said to me, "You're a horn player, what do you think of our Holton horn?" I replied, undiplomatically, "I think it's one of the worst horns I've ever played."

Instead of getting mad, they looked at each other and grinned. "Well," one of them said, "I guess that's the reason why we only sold eight last year." They then asked me to design a horn for them. I had already thought out and planned to make a horn in 1941 with the Buescher Company, but when the war came along they stopped making musical instruments and applied themselves to producing submarine compasses. The whole project went out the window but stayed in my mind. I had a simple idea: take the good qualities of each of the famous horns I owned and eliminate the bad ones. Then add the right bore and taper and design it so it felt comfortable in the hands, a point that other horn makers never paid any attention to. In the end we had a hybrid that had the good qualities of the Alexander, the Kruspe, the Geyer, the Schmidt, and several others. I won't say it's perfect, but it is now the best selling horn in the country, close to 3,000 a year.

To carry out this project, I drove to the Holton factory in Elkhorn, Wisconsin several times a week. Scheduling was difficult during the season, when the symphony had either a performance or rehearsal every day of the week, and the drive took two-and-a-half hours each way. On my trips I would pass Palwaukee Airport and numerous signs invited me to take flying lessons. Once I took my first lesson I was completely hooked. After I got my pilot's license I would rent a little Cessna and make the trip in 20 minutes. Since then I have owned several small planes and have flown everywhere in the United States.

Guest Conductors

One of the fringe benefits of playing in a major orchestra is working with a great number of guest conductors. As I look back I realize that I've played under most of the great conductors of my time. One of the greatest was Hans Rosbaud, who died a few years after we played under him. He was not only a great conductor but also the best rehearser. When we played some avant-garde work, he was able to hear relationships no one else could. He might ask the snare drum and flute to play together, and suddenly the piece made sense to us. Once some musicians my age discussed who was the greatest conductor we had worked for and several of us said, "Hans Rosbaud."

Dimitri Mitropolis was a wonderful conductor who was always polite and kindly to the orchestra. He had an ability to memorize scores that was uncanny. One time when he was guest conducting us, we were to do a new work by the Mexican composer Revueltas. The parts and score didn't arrive until the first day of rehearsal, and a messenger delivered them to the stage as we rehearsed another piece. The music was passed out, and Mitropolis put his face down into the score and began conducting. The next day he rehearsed the piece without a score and could recall the minutest details, including rehearsal numbers.

I played under Toscanini only once. He would never be a guest conductor, but he came to Chicago and worked with us for a full week for some type of orchestral benefit. Under him we did the Beethoven 7th, *Seigfried Idyll*, Gluck's *Iphigenie en Aulide*, and *Tannhaeuser*. He was just what everyone said; he would get suddenly volatile and then, just as suddenly, calm down. While Toscanini was the legend that he was supposed to be, I always felt that he wasn't infallible; give him a Rossini overture and no one could touch him, but with Brahms symphonies he was too energetic for the slow movements.

During the week I worked for him I played well. Later that same year the Chicago Symphony played in New York and Toscanini went to the concert. We did the Brahms 3rd and *Till Eulenspiegel*, which are pretty good demonstrations of horn playing. The next day I got a call in my hotel room from H. Leopold Spitalny, the manager of the N.B.C. Symphony.

"Toscanini heard you last night and was favorably impressed; would you come down and talk to us?" he asked.

24

I went to his office, and he informed me that they wanted to get rid of the present principal horn in the N.B.C. orchestra.

"Why is that?" I asked.

"Listen to this," Spitalny said as he took out a record and put it on the turntable; they had recorded only the mistakes of their principal horn player. Over the years the man made very few, but on the recording he made 20 in 5 minutes. I realized but for the grace of God, that could be me. I very politely turned him down.

One important thing I learned from all the years of performing in different orchestras was to always be nice to guest conductors. All too often they wound up being my boss.

Fritz Reiner

After Kubelik left the Chicago Symphony we had a year of guest conductors; morale was low in the absence of a permanent music director. One night I was invited to a party at the home of Dr. Eric Oldberg, the president of the orchestral association. When I got there I was surprised to see the guest list comprised almost entirely of principal players from each section of the orchestra. Little tables for four were spread around the house, and at my table were Arnold Jacobs, Bud Herseth, and Bob Lambert, the principal trombone. Dr. Oldberg went to each table and explained that the board of directors was looking for a new music director. He asked us who we thought would be the best man for the position but requested that we think about it during dinner.

The four of us agreed that Reiner was the man. At the end of the party Oldberg circulated through the house and stopped at our table last. "Reiner," we told him. That's what every other table said, too.

When Reiner finally arrived, it was a whole new ball game. He came out on stage for the first rehearsal, told us that he was happy to be here and then said, "Get out *Ein Heldenleben*." He took us completely apart for three hours and then put us back together. At the end of that rehearsal we sounded like the fine Chicago Symphony of old.

Oddly enough, I had met Reiner years before, when he conducted the Detroit Symphony in a weekly radio broadcast of the *Ford Sunday Evening Hour*. He had fired the first horn player and asked me to play for the broadcast.

I arrived on Sunday morning for the long rehearsal. The first piece on the program was *Oberon*. A vice president of the Ford

Motor Company would always give a short speech before the start of the program. I warmed up and was ready to play when this man came out to give his two-minute speech. He was so drunk that no one had any idea of what he was saying; he kept hanging on to the microphone, making a fool of himself. Finally, two uniformed ushers came out, grabbed him by the elbows, and carried him off the stage while he continued talking. What an atmosphere created for the delicate horn solo that starts the overture.

Reiner's First Chicago Symphony Recording

The first recording session under Reiner is forever engraved in my memory. Up until then we had been with Mercury, and now we were to do our first work with R.C.A. We started recording Strauss' *Ein Heldenleben* at 9:00 a.m. and broke for an hour at lunch and another hour at supper. All the rest of the time we either recorded or listened to the takes.

After about eight hours I went to Reiner and asked him if we could skip to the end so I could do the solo while I still had some lip left. "No, no," he said, "that would spoil the continuity of it."

We went on and at 11:30 at night we finished the *Heldenleben*; I had just enough lip left to get through the solo. After we finished playing, Reiner announced that we had to do the ending again. This time I broke a note.

"Be careful!" Reiner shouted. Everybody laughed because we were well into our 15th hour of recording, and Bud Herseth has used that as a joke ever since. We went back and did it again, but this time a note was broken by one of the other horns.

Reiner started stamping his feet, and I thought I had better do something before he lost his temper completely. "Why are we doing this over?" I asked him.

"A few bars after your solo the strings have a place that's not so good," he replied.

"Why don't you splice after the horn solo?" I finally said. He reflected for a while, and that's what he wound up doing. He announced to the orchestra that he was done with *Heldenleben* and everyone started to pack up.

"Wait a minute," he said, "nobody dismissed you yet. We still have to do *Dance of the Seven Veils*." That went pretty quickly and we were out of there by midnight.

The Lighter Side of the Reiner Years

Don't think that the guys in the Chicago Symphony were humorless. On our return trip from a long tour some of us browsed through a novelty shop while waiting in a railway station. A couple weeks later we were back at Orchestra Hall performing the Berlioz *Symphony Fantastique*. At the end the strings play with the wood of the bow; it's supposed to be bones rattling or something like that. In the middle of all this Frank Crisafulli, the second trombonist, tossed his novelty shop purchase, a set of plastic wind-up dentures, on the floor and they chattered along with the strings. Some of the audience saw it; luckily for Crisafulli, Reiner didn't.

Reiner conducted with every part of his body. He looked at the first violins, conducting with both hands; while the violas were cued with the right elbow, he would look at the winds and puff out his cheeks to indicate an attack. After the attack he might slowly raise his eyebrows which would indicate a crescendo. His beat was small but accurate; if he conducted a fast 5/8 bar, you could see all five beats perfectly.

He had a reputation of being strict and tyrannical. When trumpeter Frank Kaderabek first came to the Chicago Symphony, Reiner saw him backstage and said, "Well Kaderabek, how do you like it here?"

"I love it; I'm having a wonderful time," Kaderabek replied.

"We'll fix that," Reiner snarled.

Reiner wasn't always serious though and gave wonderful parties for the orchestra at which he was a genial host. The next day, when rehearsal started, that geniality was gone. After having a martini or so at one of these parties I had a quixotic idea concerning his small beat. "Dr. Reiner," I asked, "is it true that when you were a student you pasted a postage stamp on the wall and practiced outlining it with your baton for the study of 4/4?"

He looked a little shocked, then broke into a big grin. "No," he said, "but that's a good idea."

On another occasion he called the horns together at one of these parties and told us that he had just returned from Vienna, where he heard some marvelous horn playing. "I want us to be just like that," he said.

"Sir," I said, "they miss a lot of notes in Vienna."

"That doesn't matter, they told me that they don't care. They take chances and make music. They're not commercial about it as we are, they don't care about missing a note as long as they make music and that shall be our new attitude; we'll take chances but above all, we'll make music."

The next day was the first rehearsal of the season. About 10 minutes into it someone in the horns cracked a note. Reiner stamped his feet, broke his baton, and shouted at us, "Don't crack notes! I won't stand for it in my orchestra!" That was the end of "Make music at all costs."

Brass players have occasionally told me that I practiced too much, but I always felt I had a little computer inside that told me if I could play something enough times, the odds of me getting through it in performance would be greatly enhanced. If I only practiced a passage a few times I never felt the odds were right. Whenever I'd play an excerpt repeatedly while warming up for a concert, Herseth would tell me that I was using up all the good ones.

When Herseth first came to the Chicago Symphony he was already a star, we just didn't know it yet. He never did much as far as warming up before concerts, he'd play a few long tones but I never heard him play what was on the concert. I always listened to him because I wondered how he did it. On the other hand, if you listened to me for fifteen minutes, you didn't need a program.

The most spectacular feat in brass playing was Herseth's playing of "And the Trumpet Shall Sound." Every year of the 12 that I played with him we did 2 performances of Handel's *Messiah*, which meant that I heard him play this solo 24 times. In all those performances I never heard him so much as scratch a note, even that little place that repeats one note that gets softer and softer.

The greatest Herseth story is where Reiner was rehearsing *Zarathustra* and repeating the passage with those octave Cs in the first trumpet; Reiner never said anything to Herseth about his playing of them, he just kept making excuses to go back through that passage. Finally Bud raised his hand and said, "Dr. Reiner, is there something about the trumpet part that you don't like?"

"No," Reiner said, "I just want to hear how long it would be before you missed that octave."

Herseth looked at his watch and said, "Well, we only have half an hour of this rehearsal left, and I guarantee you won't hear it today."

Fritz Reiner

When I left the Chicago Symphony to go to Indiana University, Reiner called me into his office and said, "I'd like to give you a little going away souvenir. I have two photographs, one smiling, the other serious. Which one would you like?"

"By all means give me the serious one," I said, "nobody would recognize you smiling."

He liked that. His image was to be that kind of man and he enjoyed it in every sense of the word.

Recordings

Except for the recording of *Midsummer Night's Dream* made under Rodzinski, the recordings I am proudest of were made during my years in Chicago. They include *The Fairy's Kiss* of Stravinsky that we made with Reiner, the Mahler 4th symphony also with Reiner, and the *Pavane* of Ravel. We made *Scheherezade* for R.C.A. on a new type of microphone. R.C.A. was proud of this performance and invited the entire symphony to a cocktail party in their offices. We were seated in a large room where they had 15 to 20 speakers. When they turned the thing on full blast and you shut your eyes, you thought you were hearing a live orchestra. This was considered a milestone in audio technology.

I made quite a few recordings with the Boston Symphony but those were made in the 78 days. I'm not particularly fond of any of them. The real favorites of mine are those that I made with the Chicago Symphony Woodwind Quintet. Those were made on Audiophile records, and we did just about everything in the literature.

Hoosier

I am often asked why I left the Chicago Symphony at a relatively young age to become a university professor. There were several reasons which caused me to consider such a move. As a young man, starting at age 18 in the Kansas City Philharmonic, I had few health problems and prided myself on never missing a rehearsal or concert in the first 20 years of my professional career. As time went by, it seemed that every year I would come down with a heavy cold or even the flu and miss a couple of concerts or rehearsals.

My doctor suggested I consider a career that would be less stressful, emphasizing that this was not urgent but should be considered for the future. One Thursday afternoon I got a phone call from a man who identified himself as Dean Wilfred Bain of Indiana University School of Music. I always took a nap in the afternoon before the Thursday night concert, so he woke me from a sound sleep. "We have a horn opening on our faculty and would like to know if you would submit your suggestions for someone to fill it." I gave him a few names and thought no more of it.

The next week, at the same time, he woke me from another sound sleep. "You know," he said, "I appreciate you giving me those suggestions, but I was hoping you would consider it for yourself."

I had never considered such a move, but wasn't opposed to talking about it. He asked me a few questions about my present salary and told me he would get back to me. A week later he woke me again. "This is Wilfred Bain," he said, "I have talked to the authorities, and we will match your present symphony salary. In addition, we will offer you benefits that the symphony can't."

I couldn't sleep any more that day. I went downstairs for dinner and my wife asked, "What's the matter? You look a little pale."

"I think we just left the Chicago Symphony," I told her.

I did much deliberating and soul searching with my entire family. Fresh in my mind was the fact that some of the great artists of my youth had gradually deteriorated in their playing ability until younger players no longer viewed them with respect. The great artists I admired were no longer in their prime, yet many of them continued to play. I realized that I would rather quit at my peak, even if it were five years too soon, than to play five minutes too long.

The 1959-1960 season had been a good one for me, and I decided this was the proper time. I was only 46 years old and still young enough to be useful as a teacher for many years. I could leave the symphony with the feeling that I had played very well for the last several seasons, and there would be no doubt that I had left of my own volition.

In September of 1960 I joined the faculty of Indiana University and enjoyed a career in which I saw many of my students become mature and successful professional musicians. When I was in the symphony it was required that I play Ravinia in the summer; now that I had quit, I was able to have my summers free to do whatever I wanted. One of the invitations I received was from the Aspen Music Festival. Immediately after moving to Bloomington in June, we packed up the car with kids, dog and luggage and headed for Aspen. I played principal horn there every summer for the next 17 years.

One thing I considered most important about my job at Indiana was I still had opportunities to play. The school had organized a woodwind quintet and I was the new horn player. It was called the American Woodwind Quintet, and we actually got credit on our teaching time for our rehearsals. I was given five hours a week off my teaching load for our twice-weekly, two-and-a-half hour rehearsals. Every month we gave a two hour concert. With the limited woodwind quintet literature, it didn't take us long to get through everything. Luckily, every four years we had a new bunch of students and we would start all over again. I can say with pride that a number of important composers wrote works for our group and these are now part of the standard woodwind quintet repertoire.

For a while after joining Indiana University, I had problems adjusting after being in the symphony world for so many years. One afternoon I got a phone call from the Chicago Symphony; the first horn was leaving and they wanted to know if I would come back as principal. Within an hour I got a call from Dean Howerton at Northwestern University who said, "There's a rumor that you might come back, and we want you to know that your old position at Northwestern is still open for you."

A few hours later a friend called from Chicago to tell me that there was a for sale sign on my old house in Evanston. I told the kids at dinner that I could get my job back at the symphony and Northwestern and we could even have our old house back. My oldest daughter, Carol, was sitting at the other end of the table and didn't even look up from her food. "Daddy," she said, "will you phone us sometimes?" At that point I knew I was going to be a Hoosier.

While at Aspen a good friend of mine, Bill Robinson, who was the horn teacher at Florida State University in Tallahassee, dropped in one night. Over dinner and several martinis he suggested that we have a gathering to be called a horn workshop. I didn't understand. He told me that the summer before there was a string bass workshop at the University of Wisconsin and 400 bass players showed up; I laughed at the thought of 400 guys with bass fiddles running around the Madison airport. He told me that it was highly successful and if bass players can do it, we should be able to do it with horns.

I thought it was a great idea but suggested that we hold it at Florida State; I didn't want to experiment with it in Bloomington. The first International Horn Workshop was held in Talahassee in June 1969, and it was so successful that I suggested that we move it to Indiana, because Tallahasee wasn't exactly the easiest place to reach if you were coming from Seattle.

The fourth International Horn Workshop was held at Indiana University during the summer of 1972 and lasted a week. Some 350 horn players from all over the country, as well as a few Europeans and Australians showed up. It was enormously successful, and in 1980 the attendance climbed to 520. The final concert started at 8:00 p.m. and went on until 1:00 a.m. In 1984 we had one in conjunction with the International Brass Congress, again at Indiana University.

While at Indiana I recorded a solo album, under discouraging conditions. The engineer, Robert Buchsbaum, also the owner of Coronet Record Company, gave me only two weeks notice for the recording date and said he could only stay for two days. My accompanist, Marian Hall, agreed to rehearse the week before the recording date, but a death in her family prevented this and we began recording with absolutely no rehearsal. Whatever was good we kept, whatever wasn't we did over. It took seven hours the first day and finally I couldn't go on. The next day was worse as we went eight hours, again until I couldn't continue. The thing that I least like about my playing on that record is my low register. When I get tired, that is what goes first, contrary to most hornists' problems. I got through the two days of recording and the end product is acceptable, but every time I play that record the conditions under which we recorded come to mind and take away any enjoyment I might otherwise have had.

Marvin Howe, and old friend of mine, was the horn teacher at Eastern Michigan University, and at his urging they gave me an honorary doctorate degree at their 1979 graduation. In 1980 I was notified that I was being considered for a distinguished professorship, the highest academic rank at Indiana University. Harvey Phillips was the chairman of the committee and asked that I submit names of anyone who could say anything nice about me, not including my family. I'm happy to say that many important musicians cooperated with letters, including Ormandy, Dorati, Solti, and Leinsdorf.

Finally, after 22 years of teaching at Indiana University, I was elevated to the rank of distinguished professor. My new title didn't effect my teaching or way of life. It was a great honor, but true to human nature, I wonder what took them so long to give it to me.

When I look back over my years in music, I am most proud of the fact that I have nurtured young horn players to musical adulthood and now perform in orchestras all over the world. This is the reward of spending one's life in music; first as a student, then as a performer, and finally, the crowning touch, as a teacher.

PHiL FARKAS AND THE Lufthorn

Jim Nicholas

Chapter Two

Comments, Letters, and Anecdotes

Phil Farkas, age 25 Principal Horn, Chicago Symphony Orchestra

Paul Anderson
University of Iowa

I met Phil in 1948 or 1949, while he was a member of the Chicago Symphony Orchestra, and I knew of his reputation as a performer and section leader.

I was a senior in college and wanted to benefit from the experience of studying with a recognized authority. I was prepared for the worst, but hoped for the best. Was this Farkas a good teacher? Was he understanding or callous to the problems of a young student, interested in teaching or simply interested in collecting money? All these questions were on my mind at that time, but my fears faded as the first lesson began. Phil took this naive student seriously. The lesson was long and intense; his explanations were clear and to the point, and his demonstrations on the horn were inspiring. Fortunately for me, his extensive knowledge of performance technique obtained desirable results in my performance. He had the ability to explain concepts in words that I could quickly translate into a mental understanding and a physical approach to performance. He also possessed a special talent to quickly diagnose problems and develop remedial techniques for improvement. To state it plainly, there was no time wasted.

After the first few lessons I realized that Phil was something more than a horn player and teacher; he had a broad knowledge and appreciation of music, not just horn music, but music of all facets. He used this knowledge in teaching, explaining specific ideas with illustrations from a wide variety of sources. I also realized Phil could call upon a well-developed imagination to help improve an interpretation of music. He described images of the emotional qualities of a composition that would then help in developing an acceptable interpretation. Since having this experience with Phil, I recognize that many of our finest teachers have this same highly developed sense of imagination and use it to good advantage in their teaching.

Sometime during that first year of study, I discovered that Phil was honestly interested in all his students, not only as horn players, but also as fellow humans. I believe his true greatness is the particular combination of qualities that connects his musical expertise with a concern for all the people with whom he comes in contact. The balance between these ingredients gives a blend of qualities that can only be described as the person we know as Philip Farkas: musician and teacher extraordinaire.

Close to forty years have elapsed since I took that first lesson with Phil, during which I have taught horn at The University of Iowa and have performed many concerts with our faculty brass quintet, woodwind quintet, and a symphony orchestra in a near-by city. The information I learned from Phil so many years ago continues to be a basis for my teaching and performance. His concept of horn playing is still uppermost in my mind.

During a meeting of the International Horn Society in Los Angeles, the Master of Ceremonies asked all persons to stand who had been influenced in some way by Philip Farkas. The entire audience of some 300 people stood up; I can envision the same question being asked at a world-wide meeting of horn players, and I would again expect to see the entire audience stand. What better testimony could we find to demonstrate the value and importance that Philip Farkas has had to the world of brass playing during the twentieth century?

Mary Bisson
Baltimore Symphony

My first introduction to Philip Farkas was through his book *The Art of French Horn Playing*. I was twelve years old when my horn teacher, Michael Hernon, instructed me to read it. I devoured it, and since then the name Philip Farkas was to me practically synonymous with God.

Two years later Michael told me he was leaving and advised me to study with Farkas; I thought he must be crazy. How could I study with such a great man? Why would he accept a 14 year old girl from Kentucky as his student? Nonetheless, I made a tape of the first Strauss Horn Concerto with a Music Minus One accompaniment and sent it off; I was not optimistic.

A few weeks later I received a two page typewritten letter from Farkas, praising my playing and welcoming me as a student. I was overjoyed. His letter was down to earth, friendly, and even humble, and he actually apologized for the price of his lessons.

A few months later I rode the 125 miles to Bloomington with my teacher to have my first lesson. We started on orchestral excerpts, and what he had to say about musicianship and phrasing was a perfect preparation for becoming an orchestral musician. He didn't focus on any technical aspect of my playing. During my lessons he told stories to demonstrate the music. When working on *Till* I remember how he described the opening to me: he played the first 5 notes and said, as if he were Till himself, "Hey, I like that." He then cocked his head as if to listen and played the 5 notes again; and then with great enthusiasm, as if he'd discovered something magnificent, he played the entire passage. He taught many of the excerpts and solos to me in this manner; Phil had such enthusiasm and love for the music that it was contagious.

I always looked forward to my lesson, and when I turned 16 I drove the long curving road from Owensboro to Bloomington, starting early in the day and arriving about 2½ hours later. Arriving at the Farkas house was an experience because I never knew who or what I'd find there. Sometimes there would be colleagues or professional musicians, and other times just Phil in his little cabin. Often he would share with me a letter from a former student or a recording of a friend, and I was fascinated with a map on his wall showing all the places he'd flown. He stirred my interest in flying so much that ten years later I got my pilot's license.

I studied with Phil for three years, from age 15 to 18, and during those years I came to look upon him not only as a teacher but as a father figure. Indeed, I'm sure I sometimes bored him to tears with teenage problems, but he was always willing to listen and give advice.

It was always my intention to attend Indiana University to continue my studies with him, but after six weeks there I won a job as principal horn in Maracaibo, Venezuela. This is where Phil's teaching was invaluable.

After that my studies with Phil were sporadic, but whenever I was back in the States I had a lesson or two. There was a dry period when my career seemed stagnant, and it was with great joy that I called Phil to tell him of my winning the third horn audition of the Baltimore Symphony Orchestra. I had dreamed of that day and was beginning to think that it might not happen, but it did happen, and I owe most of my thanks to Philip Farkas.

Nancy Cochran Block
University of Missouri — Kansas City

In the summer of 1965 I attended the Aspen Music Festival. I was a sophomore in college, but had only played the horn for four years and was more than a little apprehensive about this new experience. When I started playing the horn, I purchased *The Art of French Horn Playing* by Mr. Farkas, aware of his long and distinguished career.

The concepts I learned during those eight weeks of study with Mr. Farkas have given me focus, direction, and inspiration for the years that followed. The invaluable contributions to my development as a musician and person fall into three general categories: first, were the actual horn lessons; every week we worked on excerpts, repertoire, technical studies such as Kopprasch, and more varied studies such as Alphonse or Galley. His approach to solving problems was logical, and his manner was so positive that I believed I could do anything I wanted on the horn. That approach has influenced my personal practice habits ever since that summer.

Second are the experiences playing in the Aspen Festival Orchestra horn section along with Mr. Farkas. I learned something very special from observing him at such a close vantage point. I imagined a player with his vast experience and impressive abilities to be beyond the nervousness which often marred my own performances. It was startling to see the anxiety he experienced and an inspiration to witness how he dealt with this tension. I sensed his anxiety, but as he picked up his horn to play, a remarkable transformation took place. Suddenly there was no panic, but rather determination. He would play spectacularly, put his horn down or go on to play less treacherous sections, and then go through the entire process again. When I am faced with a performance with which I am anxious, I remember and picture his determination that overpowered the tension he felt; that model has been invaluable in my own performance.

Then there was Mr. Farkas the human being, warm and helpful to students. Once a misunderstanding caused me to become upset with him. I wince now as I remember how I marched to his house one morning, pounded on his door and gave him a piece of my mind. He calmly invited me in, sat me down, and proceeded to discuss the problem. We worked everything out, and he continued to be helpful and supportive when a lesser person might have held a grudge.

Since that summer at Aspen, Mr. Farkas has continued his interest and support in a variety of ways. He has given me moral support and friendship during difficult times, and has provided an excellent master class for my students at the Conservatory.

Our paths cross every now and then at various horn functions, and it is always a pleasure to see and visit with this amazing man. He is an artist, a master teacher, and a true gentleman whose influence has directly or indirectly touched all horn players.

John Cerminaro
Juilliard School of Music

I first met Phil at the Aspen Music Festival in the summer of 1964. As Phil is fond of recalling, I played the horn with an Italian cornet tone and was only interested in music that was fast and technical. My favorites were Arban trumpet studies and Paganini's "Perpetual Motion" or Weber's "Concertino." I had absolutely no knowledge of or interest in orchestral repertoire or any slow melodies.

Phil had a tough job interesting me in Beethoven, much less Brahms or Mahler; but interest me he did, in a clever manner, the way Tom Sawyer got others to paint the fence. He simply put things in terms like, "This excerpt is one of the most difficult things for a horn player to attempt..." which was of course like waving a red flag in front of a bull, so I tore into the standard repertoire, trying to prove it was easy for me.

A more difficult trick was doing something about my thin little tone. In this, his pedogogical reverse psychology again was helpful, but hearing Phil play in person was central. He played with such a lovely burnished sound that I slowly realized I wasn't even in the ball park. His tone had such resonance and maturity that the budding musician in me was forced to take pause. What I heard I could not duplicate.

In short, Phil first won over my ear, then came a tiny embouchure adjustment, next some improvements in mouthpiece and horn, and one summer day, *voila*, no more Italian cornet sound. I continued to study with Phil in the summers at Aspen even while I was attending The Juilliard School during the school year, and I still consult him before making any major career decisions.

Phil never overwhelmed a student, and certainly as a player and a scholar he had the prowess to do so. He let each of us feel we were something special. I don't know how he accomplished this, only that he did.

I think the thing I shall always remember about Phil is his modesty. As a horn player and a man, he was a giant who kindly stooped when he spoke so that we who listened somehow thought we were taller, long before we were.

Gayle Chesebro
Furman University

When I was eight years old, my parents enrolled me in the Northwestern Summer Music Camp where I began lessons with Mr. Farkas. I continued to study with him through high school, toting my single F horn on an hour-long bus ride to Evanston.

I attended Luther College in Decorah, Iowa for one year and then transferred to Indiana University to continue my studies with this inspiring teacher. Since 1958 I have played for him, talked to him about the horn and music, and completed my bachelors, masters and doctorate degrees at Indiana University.

His teaching skills are well known, he has phenomenal knowledge of the repertoire, and he is always interested in new pieces, new players, new ideas. For example, I played Cherubini's Sonata I and II for Phil while attending the Southeast Horn Workshop in Auburn, Alabama. He found some fresh insight and observation, giving a new perspective on playing the piece. Sometimes he will tell a story that he is reminded of; there are hundreds of remembrances he can share in an instant.

As a teacher he has always been supportive, wanting students to play their very best for him. The encouragement and positive attitude is there, even in the midst of disappointment. At a recent performance, I played a disappointing rendition of a concerto movement. His comment was, "You can tell when a good player is playing badly." With Phil, one's value as a person is not dependent on how he plays. He is not aloof or intimidating and respects people as much as he likes them.

Being very analytical, he has always put a great emphasis on embouchure. Breathing, treated with some nonchalance, would come naturally. Once, while talking about breathing, he divided the whole process into breathing in and out, saying, "Breathing in, well, that's easy." But embouchure is another matter to him. While I was in high school he changed my embouchure from one-third to two-third upper lip; this was the way I had naturally played, but had switched to the one-third upper to save my lipstick. His change in my embouchure was the last setting I have done, and that was in 1959.

Mr. Farkas always has practical suggestions to suit the occasion. When I was preparing a recital for graduate school, I planned on ending with the Hindemith *Sonata*, but was worried that I might miss the high A at the end of the first movement. He remarked, "So, you pick another piece and miss a middle G, what's the difference?" I played the Hindemith.

Farkas' optimism, his love of people and enjoyment of life are the attributes that endear him to others. He deserves the distinction he receives.

1947 Chicago Symphony Woodwind Quintet. Left to right, Jerome Stowell, Clarke Kessler, Ralph Johnson, Robert Mayer (seated), Philip Farkas.

Mark Denekas
Denver Symphony

As a beginner I was assigned a slot in a weekly schedule of fifty half-hour trumpet lessons taught by a fellow who tended bar after he finished with us. He had little interest in me and did not know much about the French horn. Soon I knew it and quit. My band director, visibly and vocally annoyed with me, dragged me into his office and gave me two music books. He sent me off with a terse, "Learn these." I did, and for over a year these books were my only instructors. They were *Parez' Scales* and *The Art of French Horn Playing* by Philip Farkas. For me a better title might have been Philip Farkas to the Rescue, because without any other guidance, I probably would have quit the horn.

The books helped me get through my freshman year in high school and I won a chair in the Youth Orchestra of Greater Chicago, whose members were required to take private lessons. I was directed into the good hands of Carroll Simmons, who coached me through several difficult etudes each week and frequently played duets with me for two years.

Before I left for Carnegie-Mellon, I went to Chicago with some of my Youth Orchestra friends to hear a concert of Igor Stravinsky's music conducted by Stravinsky himself. The orchestra was a pick-up group of free-lance musicians assembled for the concert. From my main floor seat I could not see who sat in the horn section, but the tone and phrasing were more glorious to my ears than anything I had heard before. Afterward, I hurried backstage, not for Stravinsky's autograph, but to learn who played first horn. A trombonist answered my query: "Stravinsky brought Farkas up from Indiana." A few minutes later I shook Phil's hand, having been introduced to him as another young admirer. This was the first and only time I attended a Farkas orchestra concert, but his tone that day made an indelible impression on me, part of a concept which is now a lifetime search in my own playing.

In the few lessons I had with Farkas he demonstrated control which I will never forget. Once while we were working on intonation, he picked up a horn from his file cabinet and proceeded to play the high solo from Ravel's G Major Piano Concerto without any warm-up or preparation. Though he may have practiced earlier in the day, he had not so much as buzzed his mouthpiece in the first half-hour of my lesson. With his characteristic accuracy and quality, he stopped every light on his strobe dead-on.

On the sad occasion of Carl Geyer's funeral service, sixteen of Chicago's leading professional horn players played quartets, four to each part. We sat in two rows of eight with the first and seconds in front of the thirds and fourths. Farkas led the firsts, and I sat directly behind him leading the thirds. We were all playing Geyer horns in tribute to the master horn builder, but Farkas showed us how it should sound.

Robert Elworthy
Miami University

In the summer of 1942, just before I finished high school, I was an excited young horn player eager to study with Farkas after having heard that wonderful tone and musicianship from the stage of Orchestra Hall .

Carl Geyer, a close family friend, gave me an old King double and said, "If you are going to be a horn player you've got to play a double horn." I struggled with the awkward piston thumb valve, keeping in mind his veiled promise that someday he would build a horn for me.

One hot summer day I took the train from Elmhurst to Chicago for my first lesson with Farkas. His studio was in Carl Geyer's shop, which was then on Wells Street at the edge of the Loop. I was a bundle of nerves as I met the man for the first time. He put me at ease with his wonderful smile and down-to-earth manner. Although he stopped talking when the "L" train thundered past, he began my lesson with a brief explanation on the important mechanics of the horn plus the harmonic series and why it made the horn so difficult to play. "You've got to buzz your lips to get a good tone and you always want to keep the sound of the F side of the horn in your ear." He then wrote down some warm-up exercises (F horn arpeggios) on a piece of stationery I still have today. The rest of my first assignment was from the beginning of the Oscar Franz Method that Carl Geyer had given to me.

Phil accepted me without an audition, but I had failed to mention that I had braces on my teeth and didn't know when I would get them off. When he realized what he had gotten himself into,

44

being a true gentleman, he continued teaching me for the summer. I tried my best but my efforts were not satisfactory. I could not play more than a few measures without stopping to dislodge the wires from my lips. Phil, with the patience of a saint, finally was forced to say that I should give up the horn because I would never be able to develop the embouchure necessary to play well. That statement turned out to be the source of great amusement between us ever since. He still uses it in clinics as an example of what a teacher should never do. "Never, never tell a student to give up the horn," he would say, "no matter how terrible he is. That person's career can come back to haunt you for the rest of your days!"

My concert-going continued while I attended Northwestern and studied with Max Pottag. Phil took me back in the summer, after I played for him and he checked my teeth. We waded through the thick Pottag-Andraud Collections and excerpt books. Week after week my mother dropped me off in Evanston, I'd climb to the third floor of the white frame house and sit down in a stuffy room for my lesson. Phil apologized for having the windows closed, but the neighbors complained about his practicing day and night. As the student ahead of me came down the stairs I could hear Phil working on a passage until I arrived in the studio. His devotion to the horn impressed me then and still does. I realized any success I might have would come only as a result of discipline like his.

In spite of all the pressures on Phil in those years he was never a clock-watcher during lessons; I often left two hours later feeling I could play anything. What a gift for communicating with people he had. During those summers I stored up all the tips and tricks like a sponge; they were invaluable in later years because the source was Phil's first-hand experience on the stage of Orchestra Hall under the legendary conductors of the world. I made all sorts of marks in my books of excerpts, and years later those marked up books were a part of my survival kit in the orchestra business. Phil will never really know how many times his words came back to save me on the stage.

While at Northwestern I made it a point to get downtown to at least one symphony concert a week. Although there were many wonderful performances, several remain in my memory as being especially remarkable for Phil. There were several flawless Brandenburg performances when Reiner had the horns seated in the first circle of the orchestra. Phil came to my rescue the first time I had to play it by showing me how to take all the F slides out of my horn to lighten it up, even going to the extent of making me a special shallow mouthpiece. His analytical, well-thought-out approach to problems taught me to use my head much more than my lips. I learned that if a player can think ahead, be very alert on the stage, and anticipate problems that might arise, he just might survive. I'm still trying to do that!

Rodzinski's final concert with the Chicago Symphony was unforgettable. I bought my tickets months in advance because I knew it would sell out. The man had just been fired by the Board of Directors and that created a highly-charged situation with the concert-going public. Symphony-goers were up in arms because the orchestra had never sounded better in recent memory. Brahms Fourth and *Ein Heldenleben* were the only pieces on the concert. The Strauss whipped the audience into a frenzy; and with an emotional "Stars and Stripes Forever" for an encore bedlam broke out in the hall. Fearing a demonstration, police lined the outside aisles. Hats and programs came sailing out of the balcony. It was just short of hysteria. Phil, with that ever-present touch of class, played the Strauss as I have seldom heard it and naturally got a thunderous ovation for his effort.

We parted company for a number of years. I went to Eastman and the Army, and Phil was off to the Cleveland and Boston Orchestras. We next met in 1956 or 1957 in New Orleans. I was first horn in the New Orleans Philharmonic and Phil was traveling with the Chicago Symphony Woodwind Quintet. At their children's concert that afternoon I heard some wonderful hunting calls Phil played without valves. The rowdy high school kids had no idea what a treat they were getting.

In the Minnesota Orchestra I "paid my dues" for sixteen years as first horn. One morning in November, 1976 I received a phone call. "Hello, Bob. This is Phil Farkas calling from Bloomington, Indiana. I want to change your life." I joined him on the music faculty at Indiana University the following fall.

Julius Erlenbach

Dean, College of Arts, Letters, and Sciences
University of Wisconsin at LaCrosse

I distinctly remember my first interview with Philip Farkas when I was twelve years old. After playing for three years, Charles Zweigler, the director of instrumental music in the Evanston Public schools recommended I study with Phil. Zweigler considered him to be the world's premier hornist but was unsure whether Farkas would accept me as a student because of my youth.

My father took me for an interview and audition with Farkas. I played for him and was asked to leave the room so he and my father could discuss the results. I did not feel particularly good about my performance and was sure there was no possibility of becoming a student of the great Philip Farkas. When Phil came out of his studio and said he would accept me as a student, I was dumbfounded. He informed me that I was the youngest student he ever had, and I would have to practice regularly and consistently to make the progress he expected of me. At that point I would have agreed to anything.

I studied with Phil into my freshman year of high school, when he left for Indiana University. As I look back I recognize that I was remiss in not taking greater advantage of the opportunity I had been given. How many 12 year old hornists could claim Philip Farkas as a teacher? I did not practice regularly nor was I conscientious about my lesson preparation. Nevertheless, I remember Farkas always being kind and understanding. Whenever I had the sense to prepare for a lesson, I was allowed to play on one of Phil's delightful Alpine Horns. This was a rare treat and provided motivation for more practicing. As I look back on it, Phil knew and understood Pavlov's psychological theories.

I still treasure my autographed copies of Phil's books, which have served as the foundation for my own performance and teaching. His performance has served as the idealistic model for me and all of my students.

If Philip Farkas had not been my early and continuing inspiration, I doubt I would be where I am today.

Nancy J. Fako
Free-lance Hornist, Chicago

In 1958, I was a junior in high school and a serious piano student who dabbled with the horn. A number of my friends studied with Chicago Symphony players and we often went to concerts. After one concert I asked a friend to have her teacher introduce me to Philip Farkas. It was terribly exciting for a sixteen year old to meet someone so famous. Phil was so cordial and friendly that on a sudden impulse I asked if he would take me as a student. He said he would give me a try.

My second lesson stands out vividly. I was assigned a Kopprasch etude and practiced what I had considered diligently, maybe an hour a day. When I played the Kopprasch for Phil, he asked me if I had practiced at all. He asked me politely and kindly, but he definitely got the point across.

When I was a senior in high school, Phil suggested Indiana University on several occasions but I was not the least bit interested. To me, I.U. seemed to be only a Big Ten, sports-oriented, mammoth state university. My parents and I traveled around the country looking at other schools but fortunately, before it was too late, Phil announced that he was leaving the Chicago Symphony to teach at Indiana University. In the fall of 1960 we were freshmen together at I.U.

During my sophomore year Phil asked me to help with a book he was writing. Although he had worked on his first book with a professional writer, this time he said he would prefer to have a horn player help him and I had the incredible good fortune of being chosen. This project was one of the most important educational experiences of my life; the book was *The Art of Brass Playing.*

We spent an entire school year discussing and rewriting all his ideas, and rewrote the book five or six times.

When it was completed he asked me to help him with the printing details. We flew in his plane to various printers and I was made a part of those decisions. I had been paid an hourly wage as his assistant, but when the book finally appeared, he flew me to the Holton factory in Elkhorn, Wisconsin and gave me a horn. I had desperately wanted a new instrument for years, but could never afford one. I still have that horn and have played it throughout my professional career.

I began auditioning for orchestras in my junior year. I realized years later how well prepared I was, thanks to Phil's teaching. He has helped me with many non-musical details too, such as how to hold out for more money! Whenever I had an audition to play, I called him and he gave me hints as to what would appeal to various conductors. I went on to the Houston Symphony, the Chicago Symphony, and other pursuits, but periodically I go back to Phil for bits of advice. Phil Farkas is far more than just a superb teacher who prepared me for a professional career. His friendliness and sincerity are well-known to everyone and there is always something new to be learned from him.

Nona Gainsforth
Free-lance Hornist, Boston

On a cool June day in 1970 while registering at the Aspen Music School, I met this charming gentleman with twinkling eyes; I recognized it was Philip Farkas by his famous embouchure. During the years that followed he became my teacher and mentor. His philosophy of life, happiness, and the pursuit of horn playing influenced an entire generation of professional musicians known to one another as Phil's Kids. He was never an angry teacher, never yelled or carried on dramatically. At Indiana University I learned that the harder I worked, the harder Phil worked in my lessons; he gave as much as I was willing to give.

His quiet sense of humor was often present. When the handle broke off my horn case as I was about to catch a plane home for Christmas break, I stopped by his studio to ask if he had an old case I could use. "Sure," he said, "take this one!" He grabbed the horn from the case and threw it over his shoulder. The horn crashed to the floor on the other side of the room. In response to my pale expression, he grinned, "I just keep that one around to do that with."

During an Aspen Festival Orchestra rehearsal a large, mangy black dog came wandering through the horn section. "Be careful what you say," said Phil, "that's probably next week's conductor."

Contemporary music was not his cup of tea. He claimed he didn't like the stuff for the same reason he didn't hang pictures of vomit on his walls. "I still love the sound of a major triad," he often said.

Our surrogate mother at I.U. was Peggy Farkas, who once told me, "Horn playing is not a profession, but rather it is a disease for which there is no known cure." How well she knew. When they traveled, she would drive the car while Phil practiced in the passenger seat; she endured his practicing during all T.V. commercials. In her house every napkin, candle stick, cocktail glass, and wastebasket had a horn emblazoned on it. During his Chicago Symphony days, she stayed home and recorded his radio broadcasts while taking care of their four children, and she made the meanest Hungarian Goulash in Bloomington, Indiana.

Soon after my graduation from Indiana I found myself launched into the world of a first horn player, and only then did I come to fully appreciate what Farkas had taught me. He had preached a professional sense of etiquette and ethics that is often overlooked in conservatory programs. It seemed to exist in many of the Farkas graduates I met over the years. "Conductors are always worried about their first horn player missing notes, so keep your stand low so he can see you, look him in the eye, and remember he is always right, or at least let him think so; don't drain your horn when the fellow next to you is playing a solo; don't ever turn around and stare, support your section; practice your solos so many times that you can't possibly get nervous over them when you're in the hot seat."

The greatest thing he taught was a feel for the music. The most important thing I took with me from his studio was a love for the music and not the notes on the page.

He was most famous for the Farkas sound. When I was a finalist for the Philadelphia Orchestra, Mason Jones commented that I was obviously a Farkas product. I took it as a great compliment and called Phil to pass it on. He laughed and asked, "Are you sure Mason meant it as a compliment?" He did.

I recall the sign that he posted on his practice house, a separate cabin from the main house, no doubt at the request of his family. On the front was a large sign with the name Philip Farkas on it, only a cover was tacked up to hide the first three letters of his first name; it read Lip Farkas. May we all have the love of life, the love of music and the deep regard for our fellow man that is so evident in his example.

Randy Gardner
Philadelphia Orchestra

As a high school student my horn teacher handed me a copy of *The Art of French Horn Playing* as my introduction to Phil Farkas. During those years and through my first two years of study at Valparaiso University, this horn treatise was an enduring companion.

I made it a point to listen to as many recordings of Farkas performing with the Chicago Symphony as possible. The Strauss tone poems, *Lt. Kije*, Brahms' Third Symphony, and *The Fairy's Kiss* were aurally mesmerizing. Having been captivated by his music and his thinking, I felt it imperative to study with Farkas first hand.

When I arrived in Bloomington as a college junior, becoming a Farkas student was anything but automatic; many more students wished to study with him than he was able teach. For a semester I bumped into him, played for him, and tried all avenues I could to become his student. Happily, in my second semester at I.U. I became a student of the man whom I had regarded as a teacher for some time. The next two years were intense holistic horn therapy for me, learning in and out of his studio and on stage while assisting him in the I.U. Festival Orchestra.

After a physical problem with my jaw was corrected, the content of my lessons was primarily musical interpretation. We worked with the Maxime Alphonse etudes, the Non-Measured Preludes of Gallay, and lots of orchestral repertoire. While studying orchestral excerpts I was pushed to understand how each passage fit into the orchestral context and to investigate the subtleties of expression marked by the composers. "Do you know the meaning of *ausdruckvall, con brio*, or *Til*'s Pranks? Do you know what instrument also solos with the horn in Brahms 1st? Where does the violin start and stop its solo? Now, play it again." This comprehensive approach to studying orchestral literature is one few teach as well.

To supplement private lessons I benefitted greatly from occasional horn section literature readings coached the Farkas way. Here he emphasized intellectual understanding of the musical content and developing of musical taste. He encouraged us to be aware of our function within the horn section as well as the orchestral whole. We learned to balance, tune, and perform in various styles, keeping as close as possible to the composer's intentions; many of these points were included in *The Art of Musicianship*. Even though he was a principal player all his life, Phil Farkas taught his students the skills to perform each position in the horn section through these challenging sessions. I carry the learning which took place in these sessions onstage with me for every concert.

To hear my teacher practice what he preached was probably the most powerful lesson of all. During the summer of 1974 I played with him in performances of such works as *Ein Heldenleben* and Brahms 2nd symphony under the batons of fine conductors, and what he had taught during the previous years crystallized for me.

The perpetual researcher: Phil photographing
another embouchure

Daniel Gress

National Arts Center Orchestra
Ottawa, Ontario

While attending high school a few miles from Indiana Universi-ty, my growing interest in music led me to purchase some classical recordings for a change, instead of the Beach Boys. You may have guessed that they were Chicago Symphony Orchestra recordings with Fritz Reiner conducting and Philip Farkas playing horn. So began our association. Later, while attending college with sounds of Farkas in my ear, I came in contact with his literary skills when my teacher told me to purchase *The Art of French Horn Playing*. Through the pages of this book I began to benefit from the ex-perience and knowledge of this man I had yet to meet. After I graduated, the draft lottery encouraged me to enlist in the U.S. Air Force and play in the N.O.R.A.D. Band in Colorado. This led to our first face to face meeting. The next day, while the Aspen Festival Orchestra rehearsed the Dvorak Symphony #7, I learned that his playing sounded more beautiful in person than it did on the recordings. How I envied those students in Aspen! During my five years in Colorado there were more brief meetings with Farkas during intermissions of rehearsals or after concerts. The most memorable was the one that led me to realize that these brief meetings were not going to be enough.

After the U.S. Air Force, I wanted to get a playing job. My wife and I decided that a weekend in Aspen was appropriate, and we hoped to catch a concert as well as enjoy the scenery. The program that evening was *Colas Breugnon*, the Stravinsky Violin Concerto and Shostakovitch Symphony #5. The concert was well played, but the horn solos in the Shostakovitch were captivatingly beautiful. In the days that followed with the sound of those solos continuing in my ears, the decision became obvious that I needed to study with Phil Farkas in person. One year after that concert the lessons began at Indiana University.

Playing in a military band for four years had enabled me to master the louder, higher, faster aspects of playing horn, but I desperately wanted to rediscover and recapture the finer points of musical playing, I wanted to learn how to play the big solos.

Before this period of study, I learned the orchestral repertoire by listening to recordings, deciding which versions I liked and copying them when I practiced. I remember feeling that the conductor had not listened to the same recordings I had. In the process of teaching me how to play specific excerpts, Farkas often showed me a more reliable method than the one I had used. He made no claims of originality; it's embarrassingly simple, but it works. Phil Farkas had played these pieces many times with many conductors. He would simply say, "Here is what the composer says to do." We looked at the page, the dots, the slurs, the words, the dictionary and determined how to play the passage. In looking back I see that my first teacher, who had studied with Farkas in Chicago, did many of the same things, but it never occurred to me that I could do it, too. On the occasions Farkas mentioned the different versions of various conductors, it was to stress the importance of flexibility.

The most important benefit I derived from my studies with Farkas was confidence. He taught me the concept of developing my strengths and improving my weaknesses to have a margin of safety. He documented this well in his first book, but it helped to hear it in person. Do you have a long, taxing solo? Don't give up after one successful run-through. Play it three times back to back, that way it is well rehearsed and won't be such a shock in rehearsal when the repetition is required; on the concert you'll only have to do it once.

Farkas was an encouraging teacher. He found things to correct, but he did it in a way that was constructive. He simply showed me the right way, or a better way. My only regret about studying with him is that it only lasted a few months. I still rely on his books, his recordings and his marks in my books, but most importantly I rely on the musical skills he developed and left with me.

Michael Hatfield
Professor of Music, Indiana University

Attending a clinic as a high school student was my introduction to Philip Farkas. Because of his legendary playing and teaching abilities, my receptability to anything he presented was there, but my lack of background made absorption impossible, consequenting in a less than rewarding experience; I left frustrated and disappointed.

From this beginning it is difficult to imagine that Philip Farkas would exert such a profound influence on my life, but as time passed I found that his words of advice, musical thoughts, and technical expertise were 100 percent true. He enjoys the unanimous respect and admiration of students, colleagues, and musicians.

I started to know Phil in 1960 when, as a member of the Indianapolis Symphony Orchestra, I learned that surviving in the professional world took a great deal more knowledge than I possessed. Whenever Phil could find time, Dave Batty, another hornist from the orchestra, and I drove to Bloomington for lessons. Phil played principal horn of the Aspen Music Festival that summer and put me in as second horn, and for the next nine summers I had the privilege of playing next to him. Listening to phrases, observing balances, learning how the horns relate to different works were just some of the things to which I was exposed.

Several memories of Aspen with Phil show different sides of the man. Once, at the beginning of the summer, he asked to see a prospectus for the coming year of the Cincinnati Symphony and in it he found the DeFalla *Three Cornered Hat*. He asked if I had looked it over yet and then wrote in the prospectus a peculiar fingering pattern for a technical solo passage. I was dubious as to the merit of this suggestion, but when the first rehearsal came and the conductor took it exceptionally fast, the message was clear. The conductor looked back and smiled.

Phil's performance of Beethoven Symphony #2 was beautiful in rehearsals, and the Sunday morning dress rehearsal found him there earlier than usual, practicing. At 3:10 p.m. he was back for the 4:00 concert, and a conservative estimate of the number of times he practiced the spots again at the warm-up is 75. The concert was flawless.

It is evident he loves his work. He enjoys putting words to melodies, taking commercials and show tunes and placing them in the standard repertoire (did you know the Doublemint gum theme is in *Bourgeois Gentilhomme*, the Miss America theme and "Bali Hai" are in the Dvorak 7th?), and extending fragments of melodies to their musical conclusion even though the composer realized the horn limit; Mendelssohn did not write a high B in the *Nocturne* and Shostakovich, in his last symphony, did not go up to a high D in the first movement, but Phil did.

Once while quietly waiting on stage before a performance of the Mozart A major violin concerto, Phil finally turned to me and said, "You know, this is one of those times that if we play it right no one will notice. If it's too soft and we miss notes that's obvious or if it's too loud we'll be out of balance. Anything other than perfection will not be right." The lesson was clear that proper balances and comfort are not always synonymous.

One of the last concerts he played at Aspen concluded with the Shostakovich Symphony #5. Very few students had heard him play in person before, and the anticipation level was high. As he concluded the canon with the flute in the first movement I could see the expressions of disbelief on the faces of some of the listeners, and after his solo bow at the end of the symphony, it was apparent that whatever any of us had heard about Philip Farkas was certainly true.

Philip Farkas, age three

Adolph Herseth
Principal Trumpet, Chicago Symphony

When a young and inexperienced person becomes a member of a group like the Chicago Symphony Orchestra, the learning process of a lifetime just begins. The process of becoming a better performer as an individual takes place on a parallel course with the development as a member of a team. The importance of playing with others is as great as the execution of a single part on his own stand, especially in the case of brass and woodwind players; one is a soloist at the same time one is a chamber player.

The most dominant influence for me was the exposure to the artistry of Philip Farkas. The breadth of style, elegant phrasing, all-encompassing technique and variety of tonal colors with which he infused his own playing, as well as the overall fabric of the orchestral sound, represents a goal towards which all of us should aspire. Many motivations propel a person to constantly grow and improve, and I believe the conscientious way in which Phil approaches everything and applies all his energy and talent points out the most productive path for us to follow.

I treasure the years I spent with Phil, being his colleague in the Chicago Symphony Orchestra was a privilege. Through all good as well as bad times, he always gave 110 percent, when 80 percent from him would have been better than any conductor could ever want.

Since leaving the orchestra, his career has followed the same pattern and made him as much a master of teaching, designing, and writing as he is a performer. I hope he will have many more years of well deserved stardom.

Many people owe a lot to Phil Farkas. I am one of them, and I say, "Thanks, Phil."

Douglas Hill
Professor of Music, University of Wisconsin

Philip Farkas first entered my life through his book *The Art of French Horn Playing*. I was in high school in Lincoln, Nebraska, studying privately with Jack Snider, and with Jack's help and encouragement I studied that new and wonderful text until it became a foundation for much of my vocabulary about the horn.

The popularity of this volume was well punctuated at the banquet celebration during the 1980 International Horn Workshop held in Bloomington, Indiana. Being the I.H.S. president, it was my job to introduce our special host. I began by asking all those who were presently studying with Phil to stand up. Next, all who had studied with him regularly in the past brought the number from around 15 up to about 100 standing. Next, those who had taken a few lessons from Phil added another 100 or so. Finally, "How many of you have read THE BOOK?" caused a full house standing ovation of around 500 hornists greeting Phil to the platform.

Regarding workshops, Phil is one of the most consistently successful clinicians, capable of talking at the student's level with well placed humor for those who may be beyond his main materials. In Montreaux, Switzerland at the 1st International Brass Congress in 1976, Phil presented a clinic, titled something like "Little Known Facts About Horn Playing." To begin this session he discussed the title with an explanation which capsulated the essence of clinic giving. He simply promised that if one leaves with new knowledge he will feel he is the possesor of important secret information. If one leaves with no new knowlege he can feel confident that wisdom had already arrived.

Norman Jansen
Bergen, Norway Symphony

I was born and raised in Chicago, which made it easier for me to study with Phil. Every horn player in the area knew of him as the principal horn in the Chicago Symphony under Fritz Reiner.

It wasn't easy playing for him because he was a perfectionist. When I thought I had practiced thoroughly and prepared well for my lesson, he would say, "Try it this way," or, "phrase it this way," etc. His calmness and intuitive approach to the problems of horn playing gave me the confidence to continue and land a job in a professional orchestra.

There are two highlights which I will never forget: the Cleveland Orchestra with George Szell was visiting the Bergen International Music Festival in 1965. I dropped in to listen to the dress rehearsal and much to my surprise I saw Phil on the stage. His solos in the Grieg A Minor Piano Concerto were beautiful. The second time was in 1979 with the Detroit Symphony and Antal Dorati; this time I knew Phil was coming. They played Mahler's 1st with all eight horn players standing at the end of the first movement. This was cause for a small party at my place afterwards.

Both occasions made me appreciate associating with and knowing a great person to whom I will always be grateful.

Olwen Jones
Queensland Conservatorium of Music
Brisbane, Queensland, Australia

In 1958, after receiving *The Art of French Horn Playing* from my teacher at the University of Melbourne, my aim was to someday study with Philip Farkas. The book made such an impression on me that I wrote to Phil to say how much I liked it, and quite unexpectedly I received a letter from him in return; our correspondence made me more determined to study with him.

In December of 1970 I finally met Phil. I was 33 years old and had been a professional horn player for almost 20 years. We arranged that he would pick me up in his plane in Madison, Wisconsin, and fly me to the Holton factory. When I asked if I could study with him, he flew us back to Bloomington, Indiana to see the University's campus.

In 1972, during a 12-month leave from the A.B.C. Symphony Orchestra in Brisbane, I began my studies with Philip Farkas. As a professional player, I didn't have any technical problems but under Phil's tutelage my ability to play expressively developed considerably. He improved my musicianship and mental approach to playing the horn as well.

On my return to Australia I was a more polished and assured performer. My teaching career developed and I based my methods on what I had learned from Phil. His generosity with sharing copies of tapes, music, stories, fingerings for difficult passages, and so on were great assets to me back in Australia. The year I spent with Phil in Bloomington was one of the most fulfilling I have known.

1955 Chicago Symphony Woodwind Quintet. Left to right, Jerome Stowell, Wilbur Simpson, Philip Farkas, Ralph Johnson, Robert Mayer.

Frank Kaderabek
Philadelphia Orchestra

When I joined the Chicago Symphony in 1958, Phil was at the top of his career. He had been there for eleven years and established a reputation as a great horn player and teacher. It was fascinating for me to sit behind him and watch him perform on a daily basis. He had the most incredible endurance I've seen a horn player have, and I never heard him tire or complain about his lip.

Phil would practice a passage to the last second before going on stage. He, like many fine artists, was a high-strung nervous type, and would practice long hours to get a solo just right. He had a good-natured way about him and was never glum; he loved to laugh.

I loved to listen to him play as I felt there was great feeling and sensitivity in his work. He is my kind of horn player and I feel I am a better player because of my association with him. He left Chicago in 1960 but I still hear his playing in my mind.

Edward Kleinhammer
Former Bass Trombone, Chicago Symphony

Philip Farkas is one of the truly great artists I have had the good fortune to be associated with during my tenure as bass trombonist of the Chicago Symphony Orchestra.

His playing has a most beautiful sound, flavored with subtle rhythmic interpretation and poetical phrasing. His personal character encompasses the ultimate in integrity and devotion to his playing, teaching, and writing. On many occasions I would reach into the top drawer of my nightstand for advice out of one of his authored treatises on brass playing.

Brass players often experience a feeling of not performing to their personal satisfaction. On one of these occasions, Phil was descending the stairs from the stage and I recall hearing him say, "If one of my students played like I did this afternoon..." etc. I know that before the clock struck midnight that evening he would be doing some extra practicing. If there was a delay or an extra long intermission in rehearsal, Phil would use the time in continuance of the quest for perfection.

Phil Farkas possesses qualities that ennoble the mind and raise the spirit of all with whom he comes into contact, be they listeners of music, students, or colleagues.

Arthur David Krehbiel
San Francisco Symphony

Putting into words what Phil Farkas has meant to me is a tough job, because words are never enough; there are so many sides that I remember.

There is Phil the teacher, and this is how most of us know him. The first lesson when he tried to make me feel at ease is something I'll never forget. Remember the studio in Evanston with horns and mouthpieces and pictures of great conductors everywhere? Remember the first time he took you through a Gallay unmeasured etude or the first movement of Brahms Second?

There was Phil, the horn player. How could I forget getting chills up and down my spine while sitting at Orchestra Hall in the fall of 1957, listening to every afternoon concert? I can remember in particular a Schumann Rhenish Symphony and a Brahms Third and how Phil played with such incredible smoothness, beauty of sound, and musical taste.

A very wonderful and frightening thing happened, and I became Phil's colleague. Fritz Reiner appointed me Assistant First Horn of the Chicago Symphony Orchestra at age twenty-one. I will never forget the audition in Reiner's apartment: I tried not to be nervous because I heard that if you missed a note during the audition you were out. Reiner held up a copy of Phil's new book, *The Art of French Horn Playing* and asked me to play the opening of Strauss' *Ein Heldenleben*; it didn't sound very good. Reiner told me he had been reading the book, and would I try those low notes again with a more relaxed embouchure. I did, and found it easier the second time. Reiner was very pleased, thinking he had become a great horn teacher by reading Phil's book.

One of the hardest things being a member of the Chicago Symphony Orchestra was calling Mr. Farkas by his first name. It took about half a year to do and a year to feel comfortable about it. The only reason I was finally able to do it was because it made Phil uncomfortable when I called him Mr. Farkas around his colleagues in the orchestra. I was called the Kid by Clyde Wedgwood and Junior by Phil and Peg Farkas.

While Phil's colleague, I got to know Phil the perfectionist. Phil was forever trying to make everything just a little better; this meant different mouthpieces and horns, trying passages over and over again until it was what he wanted. He was very hard and demanding on himself while understanding and forgiving at the same time. He hardly rested in the

62

tuttis and encouraged me to play along with him on almost everything but the real solos. One great joy was to listen to Phil play the solo movement of a Brahms symphony. There was always that special legato, perfect dynamic, and effortless control along with impeccable musical taste. What better way could there be to learn from someone?

There was Phil the pilot and Phil the horn developer. I remember flying to Holton in Wisconsin to try out prototypes. When we were ready for our return to Chicago the plane would not start and Phil began fussing around, trying to get it going. He suddenly realized he had forgotten to change the fuel/air mixture control back to rich so the plane would start. Phil was red-faced about this and made me promise to never tell anyone about this mistake, a promise I have now broken; I know he'll have a good laugh about it after all those safe hours in the sky.

Phil was always ready for the latest joke or current quip and had many of these himself. He always looked at the humorous side of life and shared it with everyone around him. He has shared his large heart and wonderful sense of humor by playing, teaching, writing and just being there for all of us to love. Thanks, Phil.

Linda J. Lovstad
Free lance, New York

I was fortunate to meet Philip Farkas during an important transition period of my life, and in retrospect, I cannot think of a more suitable individual to have aided me if I had to choose someone myself.

In September 1982 the New Orleans Symphony opened its season in a new concert hall with October consisting of touring five countries in Europe. Mr. Farkas came along to play extra horn, which proved to be the highlight of the trip.

Early in the tour we traveled through southern Switzerland on a train that passed through some breathtaking mountain scenery. After wearing myself out snapping pictures, I sat down next to Phil and got out my Sony Walkman. I put in a tape of Richard Strauss' *Alpine Symphony*, and with two sets of headphones we listened to the piece while passing through the very mountains Strauss chose to interpret musically.

Several weeks later while in Nurnberg, I asked Phil if he would listen to some orchestral excerpts. As I played for him the phone

63

rang, and a player in our orchestra informed Phil that the Dresden Orchestra would be playing a concert near our hotel in less than an hour.

"Dresden!" cried Phil. "You know who plays horn in Dresden? Peter Damm."

We had been discussing European horn style and I had spent time looking in record stores for tapes of Peter Damm. We discovered Damm would be playing a Haydn concerto with the orchestra that evening. I asked Phil, "Does this sort of thing happen to you often?" "Yes, it does," he reflected, "and it doesn't surprise me anymore because I know why. A long time ago I decided to cultivate a very positive attitude toward my life and the experiences I could have; anyone can do it."

The Dresden concert was one I will always remember. The best moment was seeing Damm's expression when he saw Phil. During the tour many of Phil's former students, local horn players, and great artists materialized to visit him before, during, and after every concert.

The following year I took a leave of absence from the orchestra and taught at the Indiana University School of Music as Mr. Farkas' associate. During my stay I took lessons once a week from Phil. On one occasion I asked, "How do you get that unique, beautiful quality of tone? What does it feel like when you are making such a sound?" He replied, "When I felt I was playing my best with the best tone quality, I felt as if the tone were coming from here," as he pointed to his heart. "The tone would seemingly make my sternum vibrate, perhaps in the same way singers use their facial structure when they sing."

I believe that Phil's heart is truly the point from which all his greatness flows. Call it heart, soul, or spirit, the love that Philip Farkas has and gives to everyone with whom he comes in contact is yet to be equaled in my life's experience.

Eldon Matlick

Assistant Professor of Horn
University of Oklahoma

Describing lessons with Mr. Farkas could be compared to spending time with one's grandfather because he was always gracious and personal. Once, I had become discouraged, feeling as if I was getting too late a start in such competitive playing. At a particular lesson I asked Phil if he thought I had an outside chance of playing professionally. Phil understood and gave me reassurance that I would do fine, adding that I shouldn't worry about what other people were doing, just concentrate on my weak points; if I did this, I wouldn't have to worry about anything else. From that point on I was determined to do whatever was necessary to not let him down.

He assigned a complete battery of etudes, excerpts and solos. For tongue and finger coordination he assigned Kopprasch, Kling, and Mueller. He used the Gallay *Unmeasured Preludes* to free up technique, cadenza delivery, and solve musical problems regarding style and rhythm. Finally, for flexibility and dramatic playing exercises, he used the Maxime-Alphonse studies as well as other material by Gallay.

Each lesson covered three complete etudes, an orchestral selection, and a portion of a solo, as time permitted. When working with orchestral material, we went through the entire work because he said that in an audition, anything is fair game. When going through this material, he would ask questions such as, "What is happening in the orchestra? Is anyone doubling the part? What is the primary melodic material?" He encouraged us to listen to various recordings of a particular symphony so we would be aware of various interpretations of conductors, solo hornists, and tone qualities of brass sections.

In 1980 after he returned to teach following an illness, the students tried to do everything to keep his emotions calm as we didn't want him to get overly excited or strained and have a relapse. After his convalescence he was more stern as a task master, driving us and expecting more out of his students than ever; it was as if he was trying to cram in as much of his knowledge as possible.

Every semester, Mr. Farkas would have his students over for a party. We would listen to various recordings and he would tell us stories about playing under certain conductors and the various pranks orchestra members would pull. One of the most memorable was when Phil had to stop the *Siegfried* call during a recording session because a stage hand thought he was practicing in the wings while the Chicago Symphony was recording.

In 1983, I performed with Mr. Farkas, Harvey Phillips, and Jack Dressler at the National Conductor's Guild in Chicago. When we drove into the city we passed Phil's old neighborhood and he described how things had changed. As we passed one condemned building, he sadly shook his head. He told us that he attended this school when it was first built and added how terrible it was how something not as old as he had outworn its usefulness. After that he didn't say much of anything until we reached our hotel.

To me, this observation was poignant; whether he was thinking about the building, other acquaintances, or himself, this comment had much significance. There is nothing that is "retired" with Mr. Farkas; he continues to be involved with teaching and performance long after others would simply quit. His zest for life is infectious and he touches all who meet him with his warm, friendly personality and helpful guidance.

Ethel Merker
DePaul University

I was playing 1st horn with the N.B.C. Orchestra in Chicago when I first met Phil, and under his guidance I learned the art of orchestral playing. The phrase within a phrase, the subtle art of each and every note, the overall musicianship that encompassed his playing, challenged us all.

Shortly thereafter I was invited to play extra horn with the Chicago Symphony and was privileged to be his assistant. From this vantage point every note, every entrance of his overall artistry was a lesson and a thrill.

While his assistant on a Chicago Symphony tour in Boston, the concert proceeded so flawlessly that the tension gradually built up, much like the tension that builds when a baseball pitcher has a no-hitter going in the last of the ninth. When the concert finally ended with the performance of Brahms' Third Symphony and *Ein Heldenleben*, Reiner stood in the wings with tears pouring down his cheeks and shook hands with the individual players as each left the stage, explaining that all his life he had dreamed of conducting a perfect performance and at last his dream had come true; the celebration after that concert was lengthier than usual.

As the designer of the Holton-Farkas model French horn Phil brought the same discipline to this task. The end result is an instrument that has won great popularity.

David Moltz
Munich Philharmonic

When I think of Philip Farkas the first thing that comes to mind is his great sense of humor, endless repertoire of funny stories, and off-the-cuff remarks. He is famous among his students for always having the last word; no matter what you might say he can come up with a rejoinder.

Farkas used humor as part of his teaching style, even his criticisms were given in a humorous way. While I studied with him I played a Conn 8D, and even though he was closely tied to Holton he never pushed me to change horns. The only time he mentioned it was when I emptied my horn on the Oriental rug in his studio instead of using the mat he had put there for that purpose. He pointed to the mat and told me it wouldn't be so bad if my horn were a Holton, but he didn't want Conn acid on his rug.

Farkas wasn't a pushy teacher; if a student was satisfied with his progress so was he. He never got nasty or yelled, in fact, he was nice almost to a fault. His patience had limits, though I remember a friend who had a number of consecutive bad lessons. Farkas never got openly upset, but as the student left after one of his lessons Farkas asked if he had ever considered taking up a science. Needless to say, his comment was effective.

Farkas is such a likable person, and because his success is based on talent and hard work, he is universally accepted and respected.

1987 — Mike Hatfield, Phil Farkas, M. Dee Stewart

Joe W. Neisler

Professor of Horn
Illinois State University

My first remembrance of Philip Farkas dates back to September, 1970 when I was a beginning horn player in a 7th-grade band. My first instruction was supplemented with the Belwin-Mills *First Division Band Method* book by Fred Weber. On the second page of this popular book is a picture of a man demonstrating correct playing position and posture; the man is Mr. Farkas.

This introduction to Philip Farkas certainly gave no indication of the influence he would have on my life. During my early years in band his name continued to reappear as editor of the solo and ensemble pieces I played at annual contests. My continuous exposure to his work helped to make the name Farkas and French horn synonymous even at this early age.

I had my first lesson with Mr. Farkas in 1977, and I learned more in that lesson than I had in three years. I had two more lessons that year, driving an 800-mile round trip from Tennessee each time.

That spring, upon Mr. Farkas' recommendation, I auditioned for acceptance to Indiana University's School of Music. I was accepted and studied continually with Mr. Farkas from my enrollment in the summer of 1979 until my graduation in May of 1982.

What makes Mr. Farkas such a fine teacher? An examination of my lessons may render some answers. Most lessons were primarily concerned with musical interpretation and style, but my first few lessons dealt with the components of a proper embouchure and some adjustments that I needed to make in my own embouchure. These changes resulted in remarkable progress and the improvement of my tone, dynamics and range. The changes Mr. Farkas suggested in those first lessons gave me hope for a future career in music.

The study of etudes, chamber music and scales was certainly stressed, but most important were the "bread and butter" orchestra excerpts and concerti. Mr. Farkas' instruction is superb in all areas, but I believe his knowledge of the embouchure and interpretation of orchestral excerpts to be without equal. Mr. Farkas believes that it isn't enough for the student to know an important excerpt and play it well; the student should have it properly memorized and know its context, i.e., the passages surrounding the excerpt and the other instruments that are playing at the time.

Farkas would go to great lengths to get an idea across, frequently resulting in rather graphic analogies. A humorous episode involves the explanation and cure of sizzling tone impurities at soft dynamic levels. Often when the bottom jaw is not lowered sufficiently, saliva will form in the lip aperture, causing a sizzling sound during soft dynamics. Farkas effectively described this problem and its cure by withdrawing saliva from his mouth, stringing it between his thumb and index finger; when spread apart sufficiently the saliva string would break, thus portraying the lower jaw's function in this cure.

One of the most important aspects of Mr. Farkas' teaching and writing is his unique ability to put into words the abstract concepts of brass playing and music that are so often mysterious and unexplainable. Much of Mr. Farkas' success has been due to his never-ending quest for knowledge, i.e., "What makes this work?" That kind of curiosity led him to many important answers and the development of improved teaching techniques and equipment.

Building confidence is very important in teaching. Mr. Farkas not only knows when to build a student's confidence, but also when to deflate an ego and give a gentle "kick." Every student responds to different motivation and stimuli and Mr. Farkas cares enough to discover and supply what the student needs. By example Mr. Farkas teaches much more than music. He is a sensitive, warm, caring gentleman, who shares himself with others. He is a wise counselor in all respects, offering advice when it is needed and can converse with anyone in any vocation. He is truly a role model for us all.

Richard Frederick Norem

Professor of Music, Louisiana State University,
Baton Rouge Symphony Orchestra

Philip Farkas. The magic of this name to anyone who plays, teaches, designs, manufactures, builds or loves the horn will always be spoken or written with awe and respect. Those of us who have had the privilege of being associated with Phil as a student or colleague are fortunate indeed! He is truly a Gentleman, Artist-Performer, Pedagog, Author and Scholar.

My introduction to Phil occurred while I was a high-school student playing principal horn in the Chicago Youth Symphony. The horn coach for the youth orchestra was Harry Jacobs, third horn of the Chicago Symphony Orchestra, who invited Phil to hear us during a Saturday morning sectional. We were all awed that Mr. Farkas had taken time from his busy schedule to meet us and spend some time with us. After my first year as a student at the Eastman School of Music, I found the courage to approach him after a concert at Ravinia Park to ask if I could study with him during the summer. He said he would find time to schedule lessons, and the next week I drove from my home in Joliet to Phil's home on Maple Avenue in Evanston and was so scared and apprehensive that I nearly turned back several times. I was convinced that after hearing me play Phil's comment would be, "Have you ever thought of taking up the bagpipes?" Just the opposite took place, and I learned so much during that first lesson that when I left his third floor studio I felt I could have jumped over any mountain, flown through the air or even hit a triple high C. The routine of studying during summers continued until my graduation from Eastman, and during my years with the U.S. Marine Band I always tried to arrange a session with Phil when I had a leave.

As a teacher Philip Farkas is unequaled. He has had the courage to share his expertise with all horn and brass players when he published *"The Art of French Horn Playing."* This book was the first comprehensive treatise on how to play the horn and teach the instrument. I tell students that, "This book represents thousands of dollars worth of lessons with Mr. Farkas for a very few dollars invested." The other volumes he has published enrich brass pedagogy, performance and musicianship.

Because Phil taught me a solid concept of breathing and embouchure, I have benefited during over thirty years as a professional and have used his wisdom with my students at Louisiana State University.

Larry Philpott

Indianapolis Symphony Orchestra
Professor of Horn, DePauw University

In 1954 when the Chicago Symphony Woodwind Quintet played a concert in our high school in Fort Smith, Arkansas, Philip Farkas gave a lecture on various technical aspects of playing that demonstrated the infinite capabilities of the horn; it inspired me to know that solutions to the problems of horn playing did exist. This is when I decided I would like to study with Mr. Farkas, although the possibility for me seemed remote.

After high school I spent one semester at the University of Arkansas before joining the Navy and going for basic training at Great Lakes, Illinois in 1956. I spent the next year at the Navy School of Music in Washington, D.C. working on my horn playing in the bands there. I had a great deal of finger technique and sight reading ability, but problems with my embouchure limited my range and held back my progress on the horn to the point that I had become discouraged and had just about given up any plans of a future in horn playing. I eventually had the good fortune to be assigned to the band at Great Lakes, Illinois, and gave Farkas a call to see if he could solve my embouchure problems. It was over a month before he could fit me in for a lesson at his home in Evanston, so I started practicing to be in my best shape.

I was 20 years old when I went for my first lesson. Farkas answered the door and directed me to the round studio in the front part of his house. He suggested that I warm up and said that he would be in soon. I warmed up for about 5 minutes before he came in. The first thing he said to me was, "I'm not sure, but I think that you are using too much upper lip and your teeth are not lined up evenly." He had made this diagnosis just by listening and it was confirmed when he looked at my embouchure.

My lessons over the next 2½ years were often hard to schedule. I would sometimes walk with him from Orchestra Hall to the train station after a Friday afternoon concert, schedule book in hand, trying to find a time for a lesson. In my lessons I played studies by Kopprasch, Gallay and Maxime Alphonse, some solo pieces, concertos, and lots of orchestral excerpts. My embouchure continued to grow stronger, which I attribute to playing the warm-ups from the Farkas book every day. My orchestra playing improved by playing in all of the community orchestras along the north shore, or as Farkas suggested, "playing every chance you get."

I learned a great deal in my lessons, but I learned as much from listening to Farkas playing in the Chicago Symphony and from watching how he approached and prepared for his work. He practiced the difficult passages until he could play them in his sleep and always prepared passages slower or faster or louder or softer than they would ever need to be played. He always practiced far in advance of a performance. I remember going to a lesson in May and seeing the score to *Le Baiser de la Fee* by Stravinsky on his music stand. When I asked if they were going to be playing that soon, he replied, "Yes, in November." That in itself was a lesson.

I continued to study with him until January of 1960, when I was released from the Navy. We discussed what I should do about my career and whether I should go to music school. He suggested that I delay school and try for a job he had heard about in North Carolina. I made a tape in his studio, and this led to an audition and a job in the North Carolina Symphony. After my last lesson Farkas said, "You play as much horn as anybody; now you must learn to play as well." While making the audition tape at Farkas' home, I moved into the living room from the studio to get more resonance and attracted the attention of the Farkas' youngest daughter, who was then six years old. She said, "If you and Daddy had a contest, Daddy would win." Farkas turned fortissimo red with embarrassment, the only time I have seen him at a loss for words.

When I joined the Indianapolis Symphony for the 1964-65 season, the opening concert was *Oberon, Till Eulenspiegel,* and Brahms' First Symphony. After one of the first concerts someone told me that a friend of mine was waiting outside the dressing room to see me. I was surprised and delighted to see Farkas, who had come to wish me well.

During my career in Indianapolis I have enjoyed his friendship and have turned to him for advice on many aspects of the music business. I have enjoyed his great success as a teacher at Indiana University and have been happy to see the progress of many of his students into outstanding careers.

A few years ago we played Mahler's Symphony Number 2, which calls for 10 horn players. One of my students was playing 10th horn, and I commented to Farkas that there were three generations of horn players from the Farkas school playing the concert. With as quick a wit as always, he replied, "That's good, but it's too bad I'm in the wrong generation!"

Perhaps I was most influenced by him in my first lesson, when he asked me what I wanted from my horn playing. Even though I didn't know the answer for certain I said, "I want to be a professional horn player," and he took me at my word.

William C. Robinson
Baylor University (Retired)

In 1953 the Woodwind Quintet of the Chicago Symphony visited Norman, Oklahoma, and played in the high school where I was the band director; that was the first time I heard Phil Farkas play in person, and I still have the memory of that beautiful, singing sound which has always been his trademark. I vividly remember thinking to myself, "That is the way the horn should sound, and that is the way I want to sound." This meeting was the beginning of a friendship which has spanned more than thirty years.

My horn playing had become neglected; the pressing duties of a high school band director made it impossible for me to continue playing. Hearing Phil play was such an inspiration that I resolved to seriously work again on the horn. At the time I was practicing three and four hours a day and rapidly getting worse, so I made up my mind to go to Chicago and take some lessons with Farkas to find out what was wrong, and either correct the problem or put the horn away forever.

I drove to Chicago and attended a rehearsal and concert of the Chicago Symphony at Ravinia. Two sounds from the rehearsal and concert are indelibly imprinted in my memory: the trumpet sound of the Promenade from *Pictures At an Exhibition*, played by Adolph Herseth, and the opening solo of the Brahms Piano Concerto in B♭, played by Farkas.

Farkas' busy schedule permitted only three lessons during the time I was in Chicago, but I hoped that within those three lessons I would find the answer to my playing problems. It took about three minutes of the first lesson. At that time he explained to me the necessity of keeping the lips even, and therefore the teeth even, for the free flow of air, and the danger of letting the lower lip slip behind the upper, resulting in a pinched sound. He drew diagrams of right and wrong in my copy of *The Art of French Horn Playing* and mentioned, "If I ever write another book, I'll put that in." Sure enough, in 1962 *The Art of Brass Playing* was published and on pages 8 and 9 are illustrations of right and wrong lip positions.

I went home after these lessons, practiced for a year and went back the following summer for more lessons. Phil was as pleased with my progress as I and inspired me to continue working and

73

making progress. He made many important suggestions, all of which were extremely helpful.

In 1968, while teaching at The Florida State University, I had an idea which seemed to be born of necessity: young horn players no longer were familiar with the names of Anton Horner, Max Pottag, Wendell Hoss, Carl Geyer and others, all of whom had played such important roles in the development of horn playing in this country. It seemed imperative, while these great men were still with us, to organize a workshop for horn players so that all could meet these men, exchange ideas, and learn something first-hand of the heritage of horn playing.

I visited Phil Farkas in Aspen, Colorado that summer and mentioned the idea to him. The idea of a Horn Workshop was discussed and Phil liked it. "Count me in, I'll be there," he told me. The Office of Continuing Education at Florida State agreed to underwrite the cost of the workshop, thus the International Horn Workshop and ultimately the International Horn Society were born.

It is impossible to comprehend the extent of Phil's influence on horn players and horn playing. It is safe to say that it would be difficult to find a horn player or horn teacher anywhere whose success has not been touched in some way by the influence of Phil Farkas.

Lowell E. Shaw
Buffalo Philharmonic

My association with Philip Farkas began in the fall of 1955 after I spent four years playing in an Air Force band and returned to Northwestern University to pursue a master's degree in music performance.

My first lesson took place following a rehearsal of the University orchestra at which I filled in for a missing second bassoon. This was apparently not a good way to warm up for a lesson as, with the added disadvantage of first lesson nerves, I played the Kopprasch Etude #21 quite badly. After that start, things seemed to go downhill rather rapidly and after much peering, experimenting, using the mouthpiece ring and analyzing, it was decided I was never going to become a horn player using that embouchure. It came as a harsh blow to an older and experienced horn player from a service band.

The following school year was forever frustrating. At one of my lessons I complained about the high A on my horn; Phil did not buy my sad story as he put his mouthpiece in my horn, started on the offending high A and played chromatically up another octave. In the intervening thirty years I have never been successful in getting within a perfect fourth of that note.

At another lesson I complimented him on the Mendelssohn *Nocturne* he had done as a final number of the Chicago Symphony telecast the night before. It turned out that he warmed up for it with two rehearsals for the week's symphony concert and then the TV rehearsal, and had performed the solo at the end of his eighth hour of playing for the day.

The rest of the year was spent experimenting, encouraging, and keeping his sense of humor as I agonized over the slow process of finding a new way to play the horn. By April I was not only able to get through a recital, but also played an audition for Josef Krips, landing the second horn position in the Buffalo Philharmonic. One of Phil's greatest jobs acting was not expressing his amazement when I told him I got the job.

Our paths have crossed frequently at I.H.S. workshops and while my daughter was a student in Bloomington. It is always amazing to watch him take a group of 250 hornists ranging in age from 7 to 70 and turn them into a musical group. His seminars and clinics combine instruction with enough show biz that everybody can enjoy and learn from them. It is inspiring to see his continuing interest in the horn as an instrument, in the playing of the horn as a form of artistic expression, and above all, his interest in people.

Eugene Wade
Detroit Symphony

It is difficult to determine when I decided to study with Phil Farkas. My first teacher, Leo Ashcraft, was a student of Max Pottag and always talked about the Chicago school of brass playing, particularly the Chicago Symphony horn sound. I made up my mind that some day I would study with Phil.

In 1959 I enrolled as a graduate student at Northwestern University and took my first lesson at Phil's house, just a short distance from the campus. I was directed into his study and told to warm up. After a few minutes Phil came in and told me he felt my upper range sounded pinched, adding that if I wanted to progess beyond my current ability I would have to change my embouchure; I was determined to follow his instructions.

Little did I know what I was in for in making the important change. As weeks passed, I became ashamed of the sounds coming from my horn and retreated to the top floor of the music building to practice necessary long tones while checking my progress in a small mirror. I discussed my feelings with the other students and found that many of them had also gone through the same changes and survived the ordeal. At one point, I couldn't play with either the old or new embouchure, but began to see the light at the end of the tunnel.

Phil gave me encouragement at each lesson and told me that my goals for the week were to develop my range a few notes higher and lower than the preceding lesson and work for more endurance. Within three months I was enjoying my new horn tone and wanted to practice at every opportunity.

When I studied with Phil, the learning experience was unique; here was a member of a world class orchestra teaching, by way of example, the subtleties of the instrument.

When I reflect on the performances I heard him play with Fritz Reiner and the Chicago Symphony, the most memorable was the concert that opened with the famous *Oberon* overture. I arrived 45 minutes prior to the concert and from my seat in the balcony I could see Phil on stage by himself, repeating the solo at least twenty times. At the time I felt the solo he was practicing was one of the easiest in the literature, but when the concert started I soon realized why Phil had prepared for it so carefully. Fritz Reiner proceeded

to the podium, and after a brief nod with a hint of a frown he turned to face the orchestra. The next few seconds seemed like hours as
he stood motionless; he raised the baton to a point level with his
eyes and then slowly lowered it until it stopped at the second but-
ton on his vest. Phil entered beautifully and the tremendous
pressure was relieved. That day I learned the perils of performing
such an easy solo.

Years later, when the Detroit Symphony prepared for a tour of
Europe, Phil was invited to go along as an extra. He accepted our
offer and inspired us to perform at our highest level. At every stop
colleagues and former students would cluster around him to renew
old memories and meet their mentor.

Phil has always been a role model for me. When he published
The Art of Musicianship I realized that what he put into this book
was what he had done and lived throughout his career. Many
details of the book were taught at each lesson and were observed at
every Chicago Symphony concert that he played.

*1949 Chicago Symphony Horn Section. Left to right, Joseph Mourek, Harry
Jacobs, Clyde Wedgwood, Philip Farkas, Milan Yancich.*

James Winter

Professor of Music, California State University
Fresno, California

During my sophomore year in high school in Kansas City, Missouri, I was the first horn in the band and orchestra. One day we were informed that the first horn of the Kansas City Philharmonic would give a series of classes at the junior high school. I suppose every serious musician can identify certain moments which were central in directing his or her life into the channels which settled a career; Phil Farkas played one concert C and my whole concept of what life must be like was transformed. In some degree, everyone who ever heard this man's tone has had a similar reaction; the sheer impact of its beauty, coupled with its incredible pervasiveness, was overwhelming. In my case, this first lesson had a life-long influence. I still find myself comparing my own sound with that unforgettable first C and trying to find ways to show my own students how to approach it.

In the years that followed, I studied with other fine teachers and got to know many of the great artists of our time. In no way would I want to underestimate the influence of these men and women upon me or undervalue the wonder of their playing, yet, there stands the Farkas tone, which, combined with his wondrous intonation, incredible attack, and thoughtful elegance of phrase and line, makes him the central influence in so many of us.

I cannot close this vignette without mentioning the delightful Farkas wit and humor, ever-searching curiosity and scholarship, patience and perserverence, ingenuity, and warmth of friendship. Despite all these qualities it is his playing and tone that have been a constant core in my effort as a hornist and teacher.

There is a whole generation of hornists who, like me, are indebted to Phil Farkas beyond our ability to express it; I am grateful for this chance to say what he has meant, and still means, to me.

Milan Yancich
Rochester Philharmonic

My studies with Mr. Farkas began in the summer of 1940, after finishing my freshman year at the University of Michigan. My lessons would sometimes range into the hour and a half to two hour periods, depending on how well or how poorly I played. I remember spending that summer on basics of the horn, listening to recordings of other hornists, and sometimes just talking about music. Each summer thereafter I would take a series of lessons from him, continuing on through the World War II years because I had the good fortune to be stationed in Fort Sheridan, Illinois, an Army post north of Chicago. Little did I know I would be his assistant in the Chicago Symphony, he would be the best man at my wedding, and we would become partners in a publishing venture; we had a long and lasting friendship.

I always felt that Phil was a horn player's player; he had the qualities most horn players would have liked to achieve. He had high standards of performance, always professional whether it was a serious classical concert or a light pops program. His playing could be poetic and exquisite or it could be exciting and dramatic; he respected the instrument for what it represented in the orchestra. His strongest playing trait, aside from his tone quality and musicianship, was his ability to blend as part of a group or ensemble. He was able to soar with a solo line but also knew the importance of fitting into the musical texture; this is a rare quality not often found in today's orchestra instrumentalists.

Besides his performance abilities, Farkas had the type of personality as leader of the horn section to foster a sense of good fellowship. In the three years I was in the Chicago Symphony, our section was close. Whenever we went on tours, even a day's jaunt to Milwaukee, we would always dine together. We had our own corner to warm up in, we were a team.

I have great admiration for Phil Farkas, not only because he was such a great artist, but also because he overcame the physical debilities of being asthmatic that would have defeated many others. Of all horn players in this century he has made a profound impression on the horn playing community that may never be equaled.

79

November 13, 1979

Dear Charles,

Mr. Philip Farkas is an extraordinary individual with whom I have had the greatest pleasure being associated during my visits to Indiana University.

He is indeed a man of exemplary character, a very talented and distinguished musician, and, in my opinion, he would enhance the status of any faculty of which he is a member.

I would indeed recommend Mr. Farkas to the appointment of Distinguished Professor of Music at Indiana University.

Very sincerely yours,

Sergiu Comissiona

November 30, 1979

Dear Dr. Webb,

Your letter of November 2nd concerning Professor Philip Farkas could not have arrived at a better time.

As you know, Professor Farkas is now with us — that is, with the Detroit Symphony Orchestra — on an extended tour of Europe. In fact, the tour ends in the evening of the very day of this writing.

Thus, I have had the pleasure of Farkas' company, professionally and personally, for the last five weeks again, after more than 35 years that I have known him.

I have asked him to join us on this tour not only for his performance's sake, but because I wanted to expose our horn section — and brass sections in general — to his influence for a while. (These sections are composed, mind you, of highly competent, thoroughly professional performers of high quality and great experience.)

The presence of Mr. Farkas worked wonders: if the Detroit Symphony five weeks ago had a fine, competent horn section, now it has one of the best anywhere, as excellent horn players of various European orchestras have stated with envious admiration.

How this was achieved, I do not know. When I asked Professor Farkas, he said only, "We talked a bit about horn-playing."

I think this little anecdote denotes the best letter of highest recommendation I could write.

By all means you should appoint Mr. Farkas as Distinguished Professor of Music. For whether you do or not, he is one.

With best greetings.

Yours sincerely,
Antal Dorati

November 21, 1979

Dear Mr. Webb,

Thank you so much for your letter of November 2nd, which has been forwarded to me here in London.

I was very glad to hear that the University is considering the appointment of Philip Farkas to the rank of Distinguished Professor of Music. I have known him since I first conducted the Chicago Symphony Orchestra in 1954 and I would go as far as saying that he was one of the most outstanding solo horn players of the last 30 years.

I can think of no-one better suited to such a high ranking academic position as yours. With my best wishes.

Yours sincerely,

Georg Solti

November 23, 1979

Dear Mr. Webb,

Thank you for your letter of November 2nd. I am very happy to hear that Philip Farkas has been nominated for the rank of Distinguished Professor of Music. I have admired Mr. Farkas for many years as a man, a player and as a teacher; this opinion is shared by all my colleagues and I think he is a most suitable person to receive this honour. My admiration of him knows no bounds as he has helped me in my playing career by his example and through his several text books on the art of horn playing. I am pleased to be able to add my name to the many who will be supporting this recommendation. With best wishes.

Yours sincerely,

Barry Tuckwell

December 7, 1979

Dear Dean Webb,

Philip Farkas is a legend in his own lifetime in the music world. Ever since I was little, he was legendary as a horn player and as a horn teacher, and I can think of few musicians who more deserve the rank of Distinguished Professor of Music than Mr. Farkas. I hope that it will be possible for Indiana University to bestow this high academic honor upon Philip Farkas, as it will be a reaffirmation of the great contribution he has made to music. All best wishes.

Sincerely,

Jorge Mester

November 27, 1979

Dear Dean Webb,

I have known Philip Farkas for nearly 20 years, and during that time I have had ample opportunities to estimate his greatness, both as a top performer on his instrument (as a soloist, in chamber music and as a principal player in an orchestral situation) as well as his immense talent as a teacher.

It would be no exaggeration to say that his name has become a legend among musicians all over the civilized world, and to my mind he is an ideal candidate for the rank of Distinguished Professor of Music.

Yours sincerely,
Walter Susskind

April 22, 1980

Dear Dean Faris,

It was indeed a great pleasure to receive your letter informing me that Philip Farkas has been elevated to the rank of Distinguished Professorship at Indiana University. In honoring him, I may modestly add, you have honored the University.

May I send you, the University, and above all Mr. Farkas, my heartiest congratulations?

Sincerely yours,

Eugene Ormandy

November 29, 1979

Dear Dean Webb,

Thank you for your letter of November 2nd with the proposed appointment to the rank of Distinguished Professor of Music to Philip Farkas.

I most heartily endorse this proposal, for Philip Farkas has created a unique and revolutionary method of teaching the French Horn that is world renowned. From his orchestral background with some of the U.S.A.'s famous orchestras and the best known maestri, his horn playing set a standard of immaculate artistry to all. On retiring from the symphonic scene and becoming primarily a teacher, his reputation has grown to that of America's number one French Horn expert. This expertise has not only been confined to the French Horn fraternity, but throughout the world of wind-playing his name is synonymous with correctitude and understanding of this subject. His many publications are of immense importance to all instrumentalists and his enthusiasm for all aspects of making music has been an enormous contribution internationally.

This would not have been possible without Philip Farkas' own character, that of being a loving human being bestowed with true gentility. It gives me great pleasure to recommend that he receive your highest academic honour.

With sincerity,

Alan Civil

"Alan Civil in Deep Contemplation at Phil's." Artwork by Alan Civil, July 1979

Chapter Three

Philip Farkas in Print

"The Art of French Horn Playing" is published by Summy-Birchard Music, a division of Summy-Birchard, Inc. Secausus, New Jersey.

"The Art of Brass Playing" is published by Wind Music, 153 Highland Parkway, Rochester, New York.

"The Art of Musicianship" is published by Musical Publications, P.O. Box 66, Bloomington, Indiana.

Philip Farkas: Master Horn Teacher

It is almost impossible to speak with a horn player anywhere in the world and not have the name of Philip Farkas enter into the conversation. His many years of professional performance and recording, The Art of French Horn Playing and other definitive publications, innumerable highly informative clinics, a model of horn that bears his name, and a small army of successful students have all earned him a position of the highest respect in his profession. We began by talking about his early years, about the time when he was the age of so many students now in our school bands and orchestras.

Can you remember when you first discovered music?

All the kids in our neighborhood took piano lessons so I started at age 11 and hated it from the beginning. But at the same time I was in the Boy Scouts and they needed a bugler. I'd had my eye on a bugle in a hock shop down on 75th and Cottage Grove, so I bought it for $3. When I got home, I found out I couldn't get any sound out of it. I took the mouthpiece off, looked through, and discovered there wasn't a little brass tongue in there like the one in my Halloween horn. Finally, a neighbor, who was a jazz trumpet player, explained to me how you have to buzz your lips. So I played bugle in the Boy Scouts for about two years, and got to like music.

In junior high school I was yelling in the swimming pool during a gym class. The teacher got mad and threw a whistle at me that left a big bruise. My folks came down the next day and told the principal I would no longer take gym class because the teacher was a brute. But the principal said, "He has to. He's able-bodied and it's a required course in the Chicago schools." Suddenly his eyes lit up, and he said, "You know, he could join the marching band. That's considered physical ed." So I went down to the band department and told them, "I'm supposed to join the band. What do you have?" The answer was, "Only a bass drum and a tuba." And I said, "Well, I don't think I'd like the bass drum, but I would be interested in the tuba. I'm already an experienced bugler." So, at age 13, I played the tuba and enjoyed it very much, even performing "Massa's in the Cold, Cold Ground" for a junior high assembly. Every day for about six months I carried the instrument

This article is reprinted from the April 1979 issue of *The Instrumentalist* back and forth to school on the streetcar. One day the streetcar conductor stopped me and said, "You can't bring this on board anymore, you're blocking traffic." I was crestfallen, and asked, "What would you allow me to bring on board?" He saw a group of other band kids waiting for the streetcar, and said, "One of *them*," as he pointed to a horn case. So I went down to Lyon & Healy's and rented "one of them." It was a fine old Schmidt horn that would now be worth $2000, but in 1927 I rented it for $3 a month. I fell in love with the instrument and soon knew that I wanted to be a professional horn player.

Was there any particular moment of discovery you remember? Any cold chills?

Yes, when I heard the horns on a Sears Roebuck *Silvertone* recording of Creatore's band playing *William Tell Overture*, the thrilling climax we know now as "Hi-O Silver." At that moment my dad said, "Why don't you consider the horn? You like the sound of it." And I did. I was excited by it at that very moment. Up until then I'd been considering the horn only because of its size and because of what the streetcar conductor had told me.

Were your parents musicians?

No, my dad had an advertising business. Nobody in our family could even whistle a tune as far as I know. They tell me that I had a great-great aunt who was the first "Merry Widow" in the Franz Lehar production back in Vienna, but that was never substantiated.

Is the family background Austrian?

No, the name is Hungarian ("wolf") and my father was born in Budapest. At the age of four he moved to Vienna, then to America at age eight. He learned the English language so well that he put himself through a civil engineering degree at Purdue University writing short stories and novels for the old *Adventure* magazine.

Was he the one with the record collection including Creatore?

No, I bought that myself. Somebody had told me, "If you've never heard *William Tell* you haven't lived." The second record I bought was the "Nocturne" from *Midsummer Night's Dream* with the famous Bruno Jaenecke playing and Toscanini conducting. So my tastes were improving rapidly.

Who put you onto these things? The school band director?

He was the one who sparked my enthusiasm. Jimmy Sylvester, a very fine trumpet player, was my band director at Hirsch Junior High School on the south side of Chicago. In high school I started studying privately with Louis Dufrasne, the first horn with Mary Garden's Chicago Opera Company. I was also a member of the Civic Orchestra, which is the training orchestra for the Chicago Symphony. Mr. Dufrasne was a fine teacher. With only four years of study from the time I started until I became first horn in Kansas City meant that I must have made some good progress, and I owe it all to him. Three years later the Chicago Symphony had a vacancy on first horn. Because they knew me as a student in the Civic Orchestra and they knew I had some potential, I came back to Chicago at age 21 as first horn.

Just what does it take to be a fine horn player?

I've narrowed it down to three things: (1) the technique to play any music, or any musical ideas that come to your mind, (2) the musicianship to have good things come to your mind, and (3) the courage to play in public. I know so many students who play well in their lessons and then panic when they get in front of a crowd. The one simple solution to that problem is to perform more often. Familiarity doesn't breed contempt in this case; it breeds courage. I remember my first year in the Chicago Symphony. I was only 21, playing first horn, and I remember that sea of faces frightening me so much the first year. By the second year I began to look around: there's the lady who falls asleep in the slow movements, and that's the one with the jangling bracelets, and there's the one who knits all the time.

So the fear comes from the audience more than the conductor?

Well, no, not when we got Reiner. With him, the rehearsals, strangely enough, were the hard part. In the rehearsal Reiner would stop and lay you low with epithets. On a concert you knew he was not going to stop. And since he couldn't stop, he couldn't say anything. The concerts were actually a relief after rehearsals. I had a series of probably the most difficult conductors in the world: Artur Rodzinski, Fritz Reiner, Serge Koussevitsky, and George

Szell, all notoriously tough men. On the other hand, they were great musicians; and perhaps the reason why they were great is because they were tough. Or perhaps they were tough because they were great. I don't know which it was, but they demanded a lot.

Have you figured it out since then? Which way is it?

I think it's a little of each. One time Dr. Rodzinski was asked, "Why are conductors such S.O.B.'s?" He replied, "Well, show me a conductor who isn't an S.O.B., and I'll show you a man who isn't a conductor." That was his idea. I think the truth is that some of the section players need this kind of encouragement from the conductor. The soloists always want to play well. I've played with as much energy and effort and desire to succeed on a children's concert as I did on any other concert for this reason: if I had played the children's concert badly, the next night at an important concert with Claudia Cassidy [an especially tough critic] in the audience, I would be nervous because I would remember how badly I had played the day before. So it was always essential to me to play well regardless of who was there, and I think this is true of anyone on a solo part. Even practicing at home I would get quite shook up if I missed something, because there was always the thought, if this happened at the concert, what would happen to me? I always strived to do something that was not only musical, but also built up my confidence so I knew I could perform the music in public. This is also one of my basic beliefs in teaching: repetition is the only way to get a passage down well. Most musicians will agree to this, but to horn players it's particularly important because we have an instrument that's notoriously treacherous. I like to play a passage so many times that I literally feel I've put a groove in the gray matter and a groove in my lips and that if I were sitting on the back of a bouncing truck, I'd still be able to play that passage. In other words, I like to woodshed a passage so much that I feel the odds are in my favor; I want to think that it would be more difficult to miss a note than it would be to play it right. It's the same principle as putting a white rat in a maze and making him find his dinner at the other end. With enough repetitions, he'll learn the direct route. It's the same idea with the horn. Practicing actually consists of trial and error. First performances are the first trials and they have something wrong with them. Until you eliminate all of the wrong things in a musical passage, you aren't really rehearsing, you're only experimenting. It isn't until you play it well that you're ready to practice. I've often told my students, "Every time you miss a passage in preparation, that's not practicing it; when you finally get it right, then you can begin to practice it." So many students believe that after they finally perform a passage well once they can go on to the next thing. I tell them, "You've just done it five ways wrong for me; now you've done it right just once and you think you're entitled to go ahead to the next passage. The odds are 5 to 1 that you're going to miss it the next time, and even a compulsive gambler wouldn't go along with those odds."

Once you get these "grooves in the gray matter," is there any danger of becoming overconfident?

I don't think horn players get overconfident, but I suppose there is a danger. For instance on a concert sometimes I must play a very difficult passage and I have no confidence at all except for the fact that I played it 100 times yesterday and got it right every time. That gives me the courage to go ahead and play it, but not with great confidence, just with sheer grit you might say. And then, after I get it, I say, "Oh, now that difficult part of the evening is over." Then I'll have a simple note in the middle register to attack, and my overconfidence shows. I'll blurp the easiest note on the same concert that I got the most difficult things. In that way we have to be careful. I think playing the horn is very much like working with tigers or lions in the circus. You'll notice that the trainer never turns his back on the animals, even though they seem to be well-trained. It's the same with the horn, the moment you think you've got the thing mastered is when it'll turn and bite you. And if it happens in front of 2,000 people and a critic, then it's bad. If it happens at home, it does something to your ego, or at least to your confidence.

What about horn players' egos? Are horn players nice people?

I think so. In fact, I believe there's almost a character that goes with each instrument. Viola players are notoriously dignified. They're the ones who wear a necktie and smoke a pipe in a deliberate manner. Violinists have the wild hairdos and the T-shirts. Bass players are inclined to be a little kooky. The horn players, I think, are closer to the dignified side. If they hadn't this innate dignity, they would have taken up trumpet, trombone, or something else that would lend itself to jazz playing. Horn players, outside of a few notable exceptions, are completely oriented toward classical playing. Because of this, I think they have a certain reserve that some of the more flamboyant instruments don't have. Incidentally, I've heard some jazz played well on the horn, but it always leaves me cold because it reminds me of an elderly, white-haired lady trying to do the Charleston. There's just a certain dignity about the instrument that doesn't lend itself to jazz, whereas the same thing played on the trumpet sounds great.

But to return to the idea of confidence and ego, can you tell me when the necessary self-confidence becomes the ego of a prima donna? I'm sure as a first horn player you have to know that you're going to perform well.

Yes you do. And confidence breeds on itself, doesn't it? If yesterday's concert was a good one, you can go out presuming that you'll play well today. If yesterday's concert was not a good one, you have a little temerity about this one. If you play six concerts a week, as most major orchestras do, you simply can't get nervous that many times a week for 30 weeks in a row. You can't take it physically. Not only that, but the knowledge that you played six concerts last week and they went well gives you a great deal of courage. If you think in terms of batting averages as a baseball player has to think, and you miss a little note here and there, you can say, "Well, that isn't so bad. The audience heard six good ones and now a cracked one, that isn't too shameful." As the batting average idea becomes instinctive we realize we've been doing well, and therefore have every confidence that we will continue to do well. Even if we don't, we can refer to the law of averages. Max Pottag sat beside me for a number of years in Chicago, and if I'd break a note Max would say, "Don't feel bad, we have to remind them how difficult the horn is."

Do you honestly believe that the horn is more difficult than most of the other instruments?

All you have to do is listen to a symphony orchestra for a year and jot down who makes the most mistakes. It'll be the horn player every time. But the difficulty can be proven scientifically — the horn plays regularly in the part of the harmonic series where notes are very close together, and picking one out, especially in the high register, is very treacherous.

92

What suggestions do you have for school band and orchestra directors who are looking for good horn players? They don't have the streetcar conductor to say, "The tuba's too big, get a horn."

Yes, my first run-in with a conductor. First of all I have the greatest admiration for American school instrumental programs and their directors, because the teaching level is so high that many graduates can go right into a major symphony orchestra, maybe not one of the big five to start with, but one of the orchestras. This was unthinkable even just 30 years ago. When I was a young man, if the major symphony orchestras wanted a brass player they invariably sent to Germany for him. Most of the woodwinds came from France, and many of the strings came from Russia. Today no one would think of importing a player from Europe for an American orchestra. As a matter of fact, the tables are turned; I have at least half a dozen students who have gone to Europe and gotten good jobs as horn players. And this situation is directly attributable to the school instrumental programs.

Yes, I'm sure that's true, but many of us can still use a lot of help from specialists like you. You've heard many school bands and orchestras, judged plenty of solo contests through the years. What horn problems keep coming up over and over?

One of the things the band and orchestra director should be aware of is that the horn is an odd instrument for two reasons: the bell faces backward, and the hand is placed in the bell to partly muffle the tone and give it that characteristic distant sound, covered, in the woods, ethereal. If you put the horn players in the wrong position, you'll kill that effect. They should be across the middle of the group so they're facing the audience directly. Facing sideways distorts the horn tone. The stage also has a great effect. When we used to go on tour, one night we'd be on a stage with a velvet curtain all around the back. If we were right against that, it was fatal. The next day we'd be in a gymnasium playing up against a cement block wall, and then we couldn't play pianissimo. So directors should give some thought to the unique playing position of the horn and put the section where it can be heard. Sometimes when the horns cannot be heard, directors will move them further forward, when it would be more effective to move them further back so the sound would reflect off the back wall.

Should beginners be started directly on the horn?

Yes, this is the accepted way now. When I was a student, my first week on the horn was so discouraging that the band director said, "Well, forget the horn, we'll take the mellophone." So I played the mellophone for several months, switched back to the horn, and was embarrassed to find out it was no easier than it had been the first time. The mellophone is fingered with the right hand; the mouthpiece is larger than the horn mouthpiece; and the fingering is that of a trumpet. When you switch to horn, you switch to left hand fingering, with a tiny funnel mouthpiece; your hand must be placed in the bell carefully; and presto, the fingering's all different. So what is to be gained by starting on a mellophone? I don't know. Let the student find out from the very beginning how difficult the horn is. The horn student has to realize that his progress is going to be slower than say, an alto saxophone player who will have great facility in the same range. Somebody who's going to be a horn player should have good front teeth that are fairly smooth, lips that are reasonably well-matched (either thick or thin). The person must have good musical instincts because the horn is a cranky instrument; and you have to have somebody who is eager to play, because he will experience a lot of discouragement the first few months. I don't know of anyone who didn't want to give it up at first. If you can get the student over a certain psychological hump, then he'll be all right from then on.

Can other players be switched to the horn?

Yes, especially trumpet players. But not the good ones. Find a trumpet player who uses too much upper lip, one who has a soggy tone, and put him on the horn. The very thing that dulls the trumpet tone will mellow the horn tone. On the other hand the trumpet player who gets a brilliant sound with a terrific high register does not make a good horn player. Adolph Herseth [the Chicago Symphony's principal trumpet] and I used to go fishing together in Canada, and we took our instruments because as soon as we got home we would have to play concerts. So just for fun, he would play my horn and I would play his trumpet. Great as he is as a trumpet player, he had a cast iron sound, absolutely brittle on the horn. When I played his trumpet, I got a foggy, thick sound like a flugelhorn with the water key open. So if you want to switch trumpet players to the horn, find those with the foggy sounds. You can improve both sections in the process.

What equipment do you suggest for school bands and orchestras? Should they buy double horns? B♭? F?

I've given a lot of thought to that. If you have the funds, by all means the double horn is the answer. If not, I suggest two B♭ and two F horns. The F horn is the basic horn for a beginner because you're playing music written in F, and that puts you in the harmonic series of the music you're playing. The F horn has the true horn tone. Otherwise it wouldn't have been chosen by composers as the length of horn that has the most mellow sound without getting dull and hard. It's the ideal horn. The beginner who starts with that has to play a lot of lip slurs because the nature of the harmonic series requires it. Those who play the B♭ horn will be able to play the same passages much easier, progress will be faster, and they will get a more trumpet-like, open sound. So the B♭ horn will not give them the true horn sound or really initiate them to difficulties they'll have later. The F horns should be used for the low horn parts, where the F horn is in its best range, and they should be assigned to the two least advanced players. By the time the advanced players are able to play in a register high enough to perform first and third horn parts, they should have the B♭ horns. This instrument would enhance their high register, and because they are the more advanced players, they would be able to cope with the B♭ horn and still get a good horn tone.

What about horns and marching bands?

I don't like them in marching bands. Horns in marching bands usually play after beats, which means that invariably you're playing your note when one foot is in the air. You never have a good foundation. Our horn players at Indiana switch to upright altos, bell-front altos, or mellophoniums when they march. The horn is an awkward instrument to play when standing. As a matter of fact, most American horn players don't like to play standing, even on a solo recital when they're standing still. Also, on a football field, you need to play louder, so there's no earthly good in putting your hand in the bell. Pointing the bell up or forward without the hand in it gives a lot more resonance to the horn, but this is very awkward. It's just a double problem, and using another instrument is a better answer.

Do they have embouchure problems as a result?

Yes they do, but Fred Ebbs [the band director] has agreed with me that they can use their own horn mouthpiece on these instruments. There's a simple adapter. I think that's a much better solution.

How about concert band and orchestra literature?
Many students have quit the horn because of the uninspired music. Although I already had professional ambitions in high school, I would still have nothing to play but after beats in the school band, not only in the marches but in the concert pieces also. Out of sheer boredom I would practice octaves in my after beats, blowing one an octave higher; or play triplets, anything to help me gain some technique. That was very discouraging. Now the writers for band are so much better equipped and the horn parts are much more exciting. Still it's possible for a director to bring out some intermediate or elementary numbers which are very boring for the horn players. The director who wants to keep his horn players enthusiastic will pick music that occasionally features the horn.

When conducting a concert with an important horn solo, should the conductor throw a big cue or treat it more casually?
I always found that a big cue was never very nice. Fritz Reiner would give me the slightest nod of the head. There are three things that give you confidence when coming in: (1) you're absolutely sure of the count; (2) you'd know where to come in even if you didn't count because you've rehearsed it and you know where it comes musically; and (3) the conductor will give you a little cue. I think the conductor should avoid giving a big cue because it makes you look like an idiot: it implies that you didn't know where the place was until he told you, when the truth is you probably know the place as well or better than he does. If you're young and timid the big gesture might even scare you. Some of the best conductors look over at the strings and just give the horn a little flick of their finger. I've seen horn players fall apart completely and can't play at all when they get a double whammy from a conductor. So I think the right psychology is to cue lightly but look the other way. The moment you see you've got him started, pretend like it's not too important.

I don't want to put you on the spot with your colleagues around the world, but are there any players you particularly admire for particular reasons?

When I was growing up, most of us wanted to be orchestra players, so people like Bruno Jaenecke (New York Philharmonic) and Anton Horner (Philadelphia Orchestra) were our idols. Now I think many of the young people consider a solo career first and the orchestra second. In that case they would certainly have to admire Barry Tuckwell, one of the leading soloists.

What do you like about his playing?

The virtuosity of it, the technique, the beautiful big tone. The fact that he can get up and play a whole recital from memory is always imposing to those of us who are orchestra players because we don't memorize. He has a patrician style, and plays with the same finesse as a good flutist, oboist or clarinetist. That was almost unheard-of years ago. A horn player was happy to get the notes, and if he did it in tune, why, he was an expert. But now, they want finesse. And he has that. Another great name along with his is Hermann Baumann. He's very well-known nearly all over the world, but not too well-known in this country. He has the same finesse, but he has probably the most exciting aggressiveness in his playing. He takes chances, plays brilliant passages, and does them so well that you believe no one else could do it that way.

How about the orchestral players?

Well, I think you can almost say that if they're already in the big orchestras, they're to be admired. They wouldn't be there if they couldn't play.

It's an extremely difficult league now, isn't it?

Yes. I had some talent, but I think I was extremely lucky to become first horn in Kansas City just four years after beginning the instrument. In those days if you owned a horn you were already halfway in because it was such a rare instrument that whoever owned a horn was invited everywhere. Now that's no longer true. There were dozens studying then, today there are literally thousands of horn players and you have to be good to pass the audition. Just a few years ago there were 3 openings for the Philadelphia Orchestra and 120 people tried out. But, I'm happy to say that one who was chosen was one of my students.

What do you want to give to your students?

What they want. For example, some students want to go into the education field. I don't think they have to play like the first horn in the Boston Symphony, but they do have to play well enough to convince their students that they know what they're talking about. These education majors have to learn so many other things. The horn is my lifetime project, but for the person who is going to be a band director, I would rather see him learn to play the horn adequately, and also know the fingerings on the clarinet, be able to teach trombone positions, and all of the other necessary skills. On the other hand if someone says he wants to be a symphony horn player, I don't want him to play the clarinet because it will ruin his lip for the horn. I want him to learn the orchestral literature cold so he can go up on an audition and play from memory. I think there's nothing more disconcerting to a conductor than to ask for the Tchaikovsky Fifth and see someone frantically looking through his music. You wonder what he's been doing for the last ten years if he doesn't know that work. It's like examining a minister for the vacancy in your church and you say, "Minister number 3, please give the Lord's Prayer." And he frantically looks through the Bible. You wouldn't hire him. Well, the Tchaikovsky Fifth is our Lord's Prayer, and a horn player had better know it.

Have you developed some phrases or teaching methods through the years that make it easier to get across things that in the beginning of your teaching career were very difficult to explain?

Oh yes. I think I have quite a reputation for anecdotes or parables that illustrate what I want; but I've also tried to reduce much of my teaching to logic. First I think of myself as being similar to a tailor who alters clothing for a man who wants to dress well. I'm the tailor to a horn player who wants to play well. A person who is a perfect 42 regular can go in a store, buy a 42 regular suit, and come out without any alterations. But there are no perfect 42 regular horn players; and so I think of myself as the man who takes the student who has a lot of attributes but has a little difficulty here or there, who needs a little more in his high register, or better intonation, or improved staccato; and alter his playing a bit. I always have graduate students who are auditors, and I beg them not to come to the same student's lesson each week, because they will think that I preach only one thing. Listening to a lesson week after week with a student who has bad intonation, they would say that all I teach is intonation. But with others I will emphasize high register or legato; the next one may have bad rhythm and I'll emphasize that. The sad truth is that the student who has a problem will have it most of his life unless he fights it right from the beginning. So I tailor the lesson to the student's needs; I don't just teach generalities.

And the second thing I believe is that the good teacher is teaching the student to be his own teacher. When I got my first job my teacher said to me, "You're ready for this job. I won't teach you another day. Your next teacher is this job." I told him I wasn't ready to cut the apron strings, but he said, "You are done. I won't teach you. I know what's best for you. You go there." So I went and when I came to a problem — a musical or a physical problem — it was almost as if Mr. Dufrasne was sitting next to me. I had studied with him for so long that when I came to a problem I knew what he would say, and I answered the question myself. He was a teacher who taught me to be my own teacher. This is the entire object. If I can teach somebody to solve his own problems, then I'm a good teacher.

What are the signs that they're ready to cut the apron strings?

It's very much like raising a child; you know when he's ready to go out into the world and when he isn't. When you get to a certain stage, you know that he still has more to learn, but the time has come when the best way to learn is in practical situations rather than through more teaching.

You spoke of reducing your teaching to logic. Can you give an example?

When a student tongues when the music says slur, or vice versa, I point out that there are only two ways you can start a note on a wind instrument: tongue it, or slur to it from a previous note. Then I say, "Play me a G and an A in that order." And so he'll play it and maybe he'll tongue it. And I say, "Bravo, that's what I was thinking of, that you would tongue it. There was only one other way you could have done it. You could have slurred it. You had a 50-50 chance of outguessing me because you could only do it one of two ways." Then I tell him, "When you're looking at the music I expect your odds to go up to 100%."

Another teaching technique is one I learned from Jerry Stowell, who was in the woodwind quintet with me in Chicago for 17 years. He was the E♭ clarinet of the Chicago Symphony, and I never heard him squeak, yet I've heard every other clarinet player in the world squeak. Furthermore, his students never squeaked. One day I asked him why. He told me that when his beginning students could hold a long tone he would tell them, "When I snap my fingers I want you to squeak that note." He said they got so they could do it at will. Then he told them, "Now you know how to squeak, never do it again." I've used this same process in my own teaching, and it works very well. One of the problems brass players have is that as you hold a middle high note and taper it off to pianissimo, sizzling noises suddenly come in. They are what we call "frying bacon sounds." I was bugged by that problem for many years, and then I decided to try Jerry Stowell's idea: first learn how to do it, then learn how to undo it. I found that by moving my lips a certain way I could bring the sizzle on immediately. So I'd hold a long note and then begin to sizzle. Then all I had to do was to reverse the process, and I've never had a sizzle since. I have one student right now who has a flutter in his tone. It's a rather common thing. He plays fortissimo and a kind of "double" sound comes out. It isn't an overtone, it's an undertone, a very rough tone sounding an octave lower. For a month or two I tried to tell him how to avoid it. I said, "Try swinging the pressure on your mouthpiece a little over to the left...then to the right...then down...then up...then move the mouthpiece up or down... drop your jaw." There are a thousand things I could tell him. Nothing seemed to help until finally one day I said, "Look, you get this sound often enough, but it's always unwillingly and you're always disappointed when it happens. What would happen if you tried to produce it? Next week come back and when I snap my fingers you get that horrible rattle that comes in." The next week he could do it. I asked him what he did to produce the sound. "Oh," he said, "I just push my jaw up a little bit." So I told him, "Well that's simple enough, never push your jaw up again and you won't have that awful rattle." It worked.

Your book, The Art of French Horn Playing *(Summy-Birchard, 1956) is so well-known, so thorough, and full of fine material. Did anything creep into the publication that is not really the way you want it?*

There may be some things I could add, but I don't want to retract anything. I found a couple of typographical errors in the first edition, and they've been corrected. I get quite a kick out of it when people like Barry Tuckwell tell me the book is the Bible for horn players. It's a nice feeling.

You've had a tremendously successful career — a quarter century of professional playing at the highest level, recordings, books; you've been teaching at Indiana University for almost 20 years. What do you believe is most significant? What really matters?

I used to wonder what I am contributing to future generations, what will I leave for posterity? And I thought, "Well, this particularly good concert is one thing." But by the time we orchestra members have changed to our street clothes, there's a man sweeping the stage, the worklight is on, and the concert is practically forgotten. The critic's review will appear in the paper the next day and from there on it goes into the dim distant past. So it's not that. That's not what you leave to posterity. And I thought, "Well, it's recordings." When Koussevitsky would make a recording he would always say, "Be very careful. We must make this well. We're not making recording, we are making historical documents." And so I thought, "That's what I leave to posterity." Now I'm old enough to see some of the records I made years ago arriving on the bargain counter — old 78s or mono instead of stereo. So that wasn't it. And I began to wonder. "Am I doing anything in this world that I can leave behind me?" And you know what it is? It's the students. I have students who are now at Philadelphia or the New York Philharmonic, and they in turn are teaching some of the precepts that I gave to them which my teacher gave to me, and his teacher gave to him. Who knows how far down the line it will go, but it's a nice feeling to know that some of the things I believe in that my teacher taught me are still being taught to others. That's my sole legacy to posterity, and because I can enhance the gift by writing a book, that's even better. It's the only thing I leave. The records are no good, the concerts are forgotten. What you leave is your teaching. Sometimes I meet school band and orchestra directors who say, "I missed the boat. Here I am teaching a bunch of kids — some are smart and some are dumb. But if I had really extended myself I could have been in the New York Philharmonic." The truth is that what they're doing is really more down-to-earth, practical, and self-satisfying than the playing.

The Keystone of Good French Horn Playing
by Philip Farkas

Horn playing is a fine art, a very difficult art. Far from discouraging the student, this difficulty should be the incentive, the driving motive for success. Think of the lack of distinction in being a horn player if just anyone and everyone could play. Consider the weakness of character which would result from not having to fight for our progress — in any field of endeavor. Think of the missed thrill of achievement were there not difficult horn playing problems to be finally conquered. And certainly not least, imagine the swarms of horn players who would exist to make commonplace, and detract from, our own positions of importance in the band and orchestra. Truly, there is no art in accomplishing the ordinary and easily achieved. Undoubtedly Dame Nature was very wise when she decreed that all things worthwhile are to be achieved by persistence and struggle. By this simple means she eliminates the faint-hearted, the half interested and the untalented, leaving those players who survive her relentless refining process to enrich and ennoble the ever-improving art of music making.

This horn-playing art is one of Natures most jealously guarded secrets and she simply will not divulge it without sincere, intelligent, hard work on the part of the student. This hard work can be a very great form of exhilaration when the goal and its rewards are kept in mind and when progress can be observed. Study of the horn will take the student through periods of exasperation, elation, challenge, downright enslavement, but finally fascination and deep love for a noble instrument. What are the rewards for all this hard work? The feeling of exhilaration at the conquering of some hitherto impossible phase of playing; the sheer enjoyment of the sound of the music, *your* music; some day perhaps the financial remuneration, which can be extremely good, as horn playing is a difficult art, remember; the esteem of fellow musicians, who all admire the horn and recognize it for the difficult instrument it is; the thrill of making great music with great musical organizations; and finally, the unique pleasure of being, as a horn player, a member of the extremely small and exclusive fraternity of experts who carry on an ancient, beautiful and difficult art, its very difficulties

This article is reprinted from the December 1952 issue of *The School Musician* creating a bond of understanding and friendship (I might almost say sympathy) between all its members. Horn playing then, beside being a difficult art, is a way of life, a happy, worthwhile way of life.

While we are fully aware of the difficulties facing us as horn players we must be thankful for the many generations of horn players who have gradually evolved methods out of the old haphazard procedure which must necessarily have been the first players' approach to horn playing. Actually, most of our difficulties have been solved for us if we but choose to profit from the experience of others. It is my intention to pass on my many years of experience to you, by means of this article, in the most important aspect of correct playing, the proper embouchure. As I have received a great amount of knowledge from my teacher and he from his, this information will represent at least seventy-five years of learning, hard study, and experimentation.

For each theory put forward by a horn teacher there will be a counter-theory put forth by another. Some of these theories will actually disagree with each other but I believe that most successful teachers' ideas agree in spirit but due to the intangible qualities and almost instinctive processes involved, we horn players mostly disagree only in our descriptions of these theories. Suffice it to say that all the ideas expressed herein are strictly my own and will not attempt to agree with any other theories for the purpose of agreement alone. My only validation for setting them forth is the fact that for myself and many pupils they continue to work. These embouchure rules which I carefully observe every day in my own playing have carried me through twenty years of solo horn playing in some of the finest and most critical orchestras in America and it is only because I feel these rules are successful that I offer them to you.

In my annual tours with the Chicago Symphony Woodwind Quintet I have conducted to date about seventy-five horn clinics throughout the United States, which has given me the opportunity of observing hundreds of horn students in all stages of progress or confusion. Notwithstanding that there are many important elements to playing correctly, it strikes me forcibly, from this observation, that those who place the mouthpiece correctly and use the lip and facial muscles properly invariably get started on the road to success, in spite of occasional minor breathing or tongue-ing problems. Conversely, those who use the embouchure incorrectly can do everything else correctly and still sound miserable and hopeless on the horn. Some of these hopeless sounding players make such remarkable advances when simply told the correct principles that one can hear the improvement immediately. However, the majority of students have to work diligently for weeks in order to get rid of old bad habits, and then they must have patience while the newly used muscles slowly gain strength. Therefore patience is the watchword in using these rules, patience plus hard work plus the willingness to grasp the spirit of the descriptions and combine all these rules into one smooth function, that of using the embouchure flexibly, much in the manner in which the vocal chords are used, and for the same purpose, to sing and make music.

The proper study of embouchure placement and application can be divided, I believe, into four general rules and I will present these four rules here:

Rule 1, Mouthpiece Placement

Having studied, observed and photographed many of our finest players' embouchures, I am impressed that at least 98% of them place the mouthpiece ⅔ on the upper lip, and ⅓ on the lower. From side to side they, of course, center the mouthpiece very closely, although some slight off-center placement, due to tooth structure does not seem harmful. This placement has been reached instinctively by most of these fine hornists, but many have succeeded by making this placement mechanically, at least until the logic of it began to form the habit. I use this setting myself but have tried, for the sake of experiment, a half and half setting on the upper and lower lip, and have immediately found myself facing many beginners' problems, lack of high notes, inadequate pianissimo, etc. So I strongly advocate a placing of the lips *approximately* ⅔ upper and ⅓ lower on the mouthpiece. This brings the vibrating edges of the lips below the center of the circle of the mouthpiece, giving it a shorter length than if it cut directly across the diameter. This shorter length seems to produce much more finesse, better pianissimos and easier high notes because it is a short, controlled opening. The lip should be snuggled comfortably into this ⅔, ⅓ position, not perched in a precarious, artificial manner. Wet the lip and mouthpiece and jiggle the mouthpiece on the lip so that it actually nestles into the most securely seated position. Do not be afraid to play with the lips wet. This wetness actually allows for more accurate placement and finesse in playing than does the dry lip. If the mouthpiece is successfully "snuggled in" there will be no tendency for it to travel, as it will be so well-lodged into the natural muscle formation that the normal pressure of playing will only serve to keep it in place. There is a fleshy large section in the center of the upper lip, and it is this flesh which seems to want to get inside the mouthpiece rim for comfort. Let it do so, observing through a mouthpiece rim the ⅔, ⅓ position. If you have no mouthpiece rim available you can observe this position by using the finger ring on the second valve slide as a substitute mouthpiece rim until you have one made.

Let us sum up this entire lip setting and at the same time try to get the 'spirit' of the feeling. Set the rim with a quite close approximation of ⅔ upper lip and ⅓ lower lip; snuggle the mouthpiece (wet) *around* the heavy part of the upper lip; snuggle the mouthpiece *into* the lip so that it does not perch on top. It *must* feel comfortable, with due consideration for its strangeness, of course. It *must* feel secure with no tendency to slip around *even when wet*.

Rule 2, Use of the Muscles

Most of us make our first big mistake the day we first try to get a note from the horn. We are told to buzz, to pretend to spit a crumb off the lip, etc. Our first instinct, then, is to smile and buzz through the resulting tight lips. Right then and there, is acquired the worst habit of horn playing. A muscle can only contract or relax, nothing more, therefore when we smile we must contract the cheek muscles and relax the lips in order that they may stretch into a smile. Nothing could be further from the correct embouchure than these thinly stretched, weakly *positioned* lips. They will produce a sound, certainly, but it is a thin, nasal sound. Such lips will have no endurance, and they will resort to many contortions to enable the player to 'get around' on the horn.

Observe yourself in a mirror. Smile, then whistle. There! did you see the lip muscles gather themselves up into working position? *This* is the fundamental position for the lip muscles to hold while playing. This, too, will feel strange at first, but have patience. The corners of the mouth are forcibly brought in toward each other, *perhaps not quite as much in whistling*, but definitely *in*, so that the mouth gets *smaller* from corner to corner. These corners should be brought back *in* very definitely after taking each breath, which, of course is taken through the open corners of the mouth, momentarily taking the lips out of playing position.

When these corners are brought in correctly they will produce an opening in the center of the lips exactly as is produced in whistling. We very definitely want and need that opening and must be sure to produce it. With the lips puckered on the mouthpiece in this manner observe how the mouthpiece now *wants* to settle in the ⅔, ⅓ position, how the lips are now in a strong position to fend off any pressure which the mouthpiece might exert. Try a tone on the horn; note that, fuzzy or not at the moment, the tone is essentially dark and horn-like, veiled and smoothe, not blatty and 'white' as with the stretched lip. Perhaps it will be too soon to notice this result, but one of these days the increasing flexibility will enable you to go high, low and all around with barely a facial movement. Once the corners of the mouth are 'locked in' the muscles contract and relax to produce the various note ranges almost from internal tensions alone and with little or no external, visible change. *One warning! Do not* push the lower lip up and the upper lip down so as to exert pressure against each other. The lip must be formed with a slight opening in the center, as in whistling, and even the slightest up and down pressure between the lips can spoil this opening. This is the one mistake which can cause the entire whistling embouchure to fail, and one very likely to be carried over from the former smiling embouchure of which it is an essential part. 'Lean over backward' to avoid any up and down pressure. It is advisable to drop the lower jaw slightly and strive to attain the feeling of blowing the air through an unresisting opening in the lips, in spite of the necessity of vibrating the lips. Experiment by 'jawing' each note while holding it. Open the jaw slowly until the sound becomes quite hollow and airy and then slowly close the jaw until the sound gets thick and choked. Somewhere between these two extremes is the ideal spot to set the jaw and usually this setting will be somewhat more open than the average student allows.

Rule 3, The Lip Opening

Focus the opening in the lips to be larger or smaller as you wish to descend or ascend on the horn. The lip opening should get smaller as the notes get higher. This opening will look similar to the oval opening in the end of an oboe or bassoon reed, and will vary in size. It should be smaller in size for the high notes, in the same way and out of the same necessity that the oboe reed opening is smaller than the bassoon reed opening. Notice carefully that I said smaller but *similar* in shape. *Do not flatten* the opening as you ascend. This is simply the result of pressing the lips together in an up and down direction and has been warned against. The opening is made progressively smaller or larger from the corners inward toward the center of the lips. Again try whistling. Notice while ascending, that you do not, cannot flatten the opening by pressing the upper and lower lips together, but that the pressure creeps in from the corners toward the center. When this contraction takes place correctly it actually *helps to create* that oval shaped opening in the center of the lips. This opening must be adjusted very sensitively to each note and there is, with experience and practice, almost the same feeling of bringing a note into focus that one would get in focusing a whistled note.

Rule 4, The Relationship of Lip Opening to Volume

The lip opening is larger or smaller depending on the volume of sound we want. The more sound we want the more air we put into the horn, of course, and the lip opening should be enlarged and relaxed to accomodate this air comfortably. Never permit the feeling of great resistance by the lips to the passage of air. This air should get out quite freely no matter what volume we play. A formula might be made for this relationship of air and opening. The fuller the air column desired the more open and relaxed the lips. A high note requires a smaller opening than does a low note but even so this same high note will have a relatively large or small aperture depending on the loudness, which in turn depends on the volume of air going through the opening. Without attempting to go into the problem of breathing in horn playing let me make it quite clear that the amount of air needed to play with this puckered embouchure will be copiously more than needed with the tight, smiling embouchure. So be certain to fill the horn amply with air for all playing with the "whistling" embouchure. A good exercise to acquaint you with the relationship of air quantity to lip opening is to go up the scale slowly with a crescendo and feel that the lip opening stays very much the same size for all notes and that the crescendo of air filling this opening more and more is literally mak-

107

ing the ascent of the scale possible. Then go back and play the same scale, this time without making the slightest crescendo, and feel the progressively smaller opening in the lip produce the ascent. Long tones held with a crescendo-diminuendo will also give valuable help in learning to subconsciously combine the right amount of air and opening.

Most students become so embouchure conscious that they over-do it to a great degree and form an almost cast-iron lip. Relax and let the embouchure form lightly, easily and with no more effort than is absolutely necessary to obtain the notes. Air is your best friend and I firmly believe that if the average student would use twice as much air and half as much embouchure he would become, almost overnight, an outstanding student.

The change from the smiling to the whistling embouchure is the time to get rid of that heavy pressure you have doubtlessly needed hitherto. The very fact that the lip muscles are correctly doing their work, will, when these muscles strengthen, eliminate the need for pressure, all except the moderate, comfortable pressure needed to hermetically seal the lip to the mouthpiece.

The secret of success in using this whistling embouchure is to have the patience to get used to it, to develop sensitivity in the control of it, and to use it analytically. Never bully it into working. The embouchure which feels most relaxed and easy is the best. Make the air do its share of the work, and it is a much bigger share than you are probably asking of it at present. You will now be like the new golfer who has so many things to think of at once that he can hardly swing the club. Learn each fundamental that I have given until it is mastered and then put all these facets together and try to feel that each belongs to the whole as a single piece belongs to a complete jigsaw puzzle and combine them into a smoothly operating mechanism which will finally function from instinct, the subconscious, and from sheer hard, observant practice and learn for yourself that the embouchure is truly the keystone of good horn playing.

The Use of the Lower Lip in Horn Playing
by Philip Farkas

One of the more common misuses of the embouchure is a tendency on the part of the player to protrude the lips out into the mouthpiece — a sort of pouting expression which causes the inside surfaces of the lip to become the vibratory edges of the embouchure opening. Characteristically, the tone resulting from this is thick, dark, smokey, without ring or resonance and inclined to be grainy or slightly rough. It gives the impression that all the air is not being converted to vibration — and this is precisely the case.

Ideally, vibrating surface or vibrating string is set into motion by a force working at a right angle (90⁰) to its surface or linear direction. A violin bow should cross the strings at right angles. The tympani sticks strike the tympani head at right angles. And even the schoolboy, seeking to annoy the teacher by squeaking his chalk on the blackboard, will instinctively hold the chalk exactly perpendicular to the board. If he drags the chalk so that it slants backward to the contact point no vibration will result.

The same type of vibration is a most desirable quality for the brass player to achieve with his lips. If the lips are slanted into the mouthpiece by pouting, the vibration, if it does not stop completely, will be of inferior quality. This results, of course, from the lips not being held in that right angle position to the moving air stream. The cure consists simply of holding the lips back against the teeth firmly so that they cannot pout.

As in all other phases of brass playing, this holding-back feeling is not violent or intense. It is no more, perhaps, than the refusal to permit a pout. Anyone using the cheeks correctly will find that there is very little tendency to pout, as the cheek contraction, opposing, as it does, the lip contraction, draws the lips quite firmly over the arch of the front teeth. So, in correcting this inclination to pout into the mouthpiece, the player should give careful consideration to the cheek muscles and see that they are upholding their share of the work. For, if they are contracting sufficiently, the tendency to let the lips sag into the mouthpiece is practically nil.

This article is reprinted from the November 1959 issue of *The International Musician*

The Happy Mean

In all embouchure problems, over correction is as bad as no correction at all. If, in training a tightrope walker, you corrected his tendency to fall always to his right by suggesting that he fall to the left from that time on, he would be little better off. Brass playing and tightrope walking are very much alike in that a perfect balance requires that we lean neither too far left nor too far right.

From the foregoing warning against pouting, it is conceivable that some students will say to themselves, "I'll fix that problem once and for all by pulling the lips back until they curve in over the teeth like those of an oboe player!"

The result of this would be even more detrimental to good brass playing than the pout. Here is what happens when the lips slant backward even the slightest degree; the air pressure blowing against the lips tries to swing the lips out, and the little opening so necessary to forming a clear, free tone is actually blown shut. If we imagine a little pair of swinging doors in place of the lips, we shall understand why this undesirable action takes place. Let us suppose that these swinging doors actually touch each other when they are in alignment. Now, if air is forced through them they swing outward. As they do so, the edges, which were just touching, separate, and the opening between them gets larger and larger as the air pressure is increased. However, if the doors are slanted *inward* before the air pressure is applied, the commencement of the air pressure swings the doors *closed*. Thus the inward slanted lips produce the most undesirable condition of closing tighter and tighter as the player tries to play louder and louder. Players who get the feeling that the horn chokes up as they try to make a crescendo would do well to explore the possibility that their lips might be held in just such a back-slanted position.

Lower Lip Discipline

The lower lip would seem to be more often the offender. Perhaps it is because the surfaces of the lower teeth, being smaller, offer it less support than the upper teeth offer the upper lip. Or perhaps the lower jaw, tending to recede as it does, allows the lower lip to slide back of the upper lip and thus create a new bad habit. I have had success in curing this problem, once it is definitely established that it *is* the lower lip which is curling in, by the procedure outlined in the following:

110

First, we must understand that the lower lip is most remarkably agile — much more so than the upper. Its construction permits it to roll very far outward so that it appears large and pouted. Or it can be rolled back inward so that no red shows at all. Because of this we might say that the lower lip has the ability to swivel, exposing at will the finest thin red line or the utmost fullness, including even the inner surface. This flexibility is another reason why we so often find the lower lip rolled or slanted too far back. Luckily, however, this same flexibility makes the correction of the problem relatively easy. Place the lips in the usual playing position on that invaluable aid, the mouthpiece rim, and, using the mirror, observe the proportion of each lip being used. Then, without moving or disturbing the upper lip in any way, deliberately take the lower lip out of the rim and replace it lower on the rim. In other words, put *less* lower lip into the mouthpiece. This will result in too large an opening between the lips — one which could not possibly vibrate.

Now, without sliding either lip on the mouthpiece rim, *roll* the lower lip farther into the mouthpiece. The flesh of the lower lip will then fill in this too-large opening, and, with proper judgment, make the opening just right in size. Note that the lower lip is now exposing slightly more of its inner surface. This procedure might be put in another way. Place the upper lip as always, but deliberately place the mouthpiece a *little* too *high* on the lower lip; then slightly (please note that "slightly"!) turn the lower lip inside-out until the proper amount of lower lip is again showing in the mouthpiece rim. It will appear to be the same amount as always *but* the actual playing surface will consist of more of the inner area of the lower lip.

In seeking the utmost moderation in applying this somewhat abstract principle, let us keep well in mind that we are not attempting to pout the lower lip *outward* to a noticeable degree, but only to keep it from rolling *inward* to a detrimental degree. This entire concept must be tried experimentally with the utmost delicacy and finesse, lest we lean too far in the other direction.

As an aside, it might be of interest to the reader to learn that the horn players of a hundred years ago used a lip setting on the mouthpiece which required such an extreme application of this outward rolling of the lower lip that it appeared as though the lower lip was actually out of the mouthpiece and even encompassing some of the mouthpiece beyond and outside the rim. Because of its appearance, this embouchure setting was called in Germany *einsetzen* (setting in). This contrasted with the embouchure the trumpet players of that time and most modern brass players use today, a "setting-on position," called in Germany, *ansetzen*. Although this old "setting-in" position gave every appearance of employing no lower lip in the mouthpiece, such was not the case. Most of the lower lip was outside the mouthpiece, but the lip was so rolled inside-out that quite a substantial amount of the lower lip was in fact present in the mouthpiece. The proportions were much the same as they are for modern horn players; two-thirds upper lip and one-third lower lip. The difference lay in the *part* of the lower lip used. The old "setting-in" method used the soft, always moist, inner surface of the lower lip. Although this had some drawbacks, its chief advantages were an extremely soft, mellow tone and smooth, liquid-like slurs.

Similar Features

Our modern "setting-on" method loses some of this tone and produces a harder slur, but gives better endurance, easier high notes and greater technique. Though we use this modern method almost exclusively today, the two methods are not so diametrically opposed as their names might indicate. There has always been a suggestion of that "setting-in" usage of the lower lip in the "setting-on" embouchure, and it is this spirit or feeling of similarity, however slight, that I have tried to convey in this discourse concerning the lower lip.

Reflections of a Longtime Musician
by Philip Farkas

Sometimes I look at today's young talented musicians and envy them for their many years to come of playing in great orchestras and chamber music ensembles. Then I remember that I, too, am very fortunate and blessed; I have something that these young musicians can never have, the experience of playing with many of the great conductors, soloists, composers, and orchestral musicians who are now gone from the scene. I like to think that my career encompassed a golden age of music. I'm confident that the present time will also be considered a golden age, but we won't fully appreciate this until we can look back and evaluate our musical scene from the perspective that only time can bring.

What a wonderful privilege it is for me to look back and recall some of my musical experiences. Imagine the thrill I had in playing the music of the great composers with them either conducting their own music or playing the solo part. Sergei Rachmaninoff came to Chicago and Cleveland nearly every year for a number of seasons. He was the piano soloist for his own concertos; he also conducted several of his own works with our Chicago Symphony Orchestra. What a wonderful conductor he was! Even with his great talent he made a slight error with the baton at one of these concerts, which threw the orchestra off-balance for a few seconds. At the end of that movement he did something that I have waited in vain for any other conductor to do. He turned to the audience and said in a loud, clear voice, "Dot vas my fault!" That takes a great man.

On several occasions I have had the opportunity to talk with Rachmaninoff, ostensibly to ask about some phrase for the horn. The real reason, of course, was just to talk to him. Even so he always had words of wisdom for me.

Serge Prokofiev visited Chicago during my first year in the symphony and played his Third Piano Concerto and conducted his *Romeo and Juliet* ballet music. He was a tall, thin, angular man who looked remarkably like a condor trying to take off when he conducted. Still he was most authoritative about tempos, dynamics, and interpretation and gave an incredibly forceful, dynamic performance of the concerto.

This article is reprinted from the September 1987 issue of *The Instrumentalist*

113

Igor Stravinsky was a guest nearly every year and conducted many of his compositions. Although he would probably not be considered a graceful conductor, he did conduct with vigor and great accuracy. This of course was an absolute necessity, considering the complexity of his rhythms. His love for Tchaikovsky's music was always evident; nearly all of his concerts included a work by Tchaikovsky, often a rarely heard one. One pleasant recollection: a group of us from the Boston Symphony entered a restaurant after a rehearsal with Stravinsky and there he was, seated at a table. He motioned for us to come sit with him which we hastened to do. A memorable lunch with a great genius!

The great Rumanian composer and violinist Georges Enesco was an unforgettable guest. He played a Mozart Violin Concerto with impeccable taste and then conducted one of his famous *Rumanian Rhapsodies*. We also had a number of visits from Paul Hindemith; he played the viola on several occasions and I got to play some chamber music with him. He once took the time to discuss the niceties of his famous *Kleine Kammermusik* for woodwind quintet with us members of the Chicago Symphony Woodwind Quintet. Among other well-known composers I was privileged to know and work with were Leonard Bernstein, John Alden Carpenter, Deems Taylor, Eric DeLamarter, and Ernst von Dohnanyi.

What a wonderful experience it was to play in the orchestra accompanying such soloists as Fritz Kreisler, Jascha Heifetz, Sergei Rachmaninoff, Artur Rubenstein, Artur Schnabel, Vladimir Horowitz, Gregor Piatigorsky, Josef Hoffman, Helen Traubel, Kirsten Flagstad, Claudio Arrau, Dame Myra Hess, Rudolf Serkin, and Byron Janis.

What great fortune it was for me to have as permanent conductors Frederick Stock, Artur Rodzinski, Serge Koussevitsky, George Szell, and Fritz Reiner. I also learned from the many guest conductors who came during my years in the Chicago, Cleveland, and Boston Symphonies. They included Arturo Toscanini, Leopold Stokowski, Josef Krips, Charles Munch, Paul Paray, Bruno Walter, Eugene Ormandy, Sir Thomas Beecham, Sir John Barbirolli, Sir Georg Solti, Eduard van Beinum, Ernest Ansermet, Pierre Monteux, Carlo Maria Giulini, Dmitri Mitropoulos, and Otto Klemperer.

I have a purpose in enumerating these names, besides enjoying the memory of working with these great musicians. From each of these world-famous musicians I learned a music lesson, often an important one, by observing how they did what they did and what they said about their compositions or interpretations of the works they were playing. Here was a cross-section of the musical beliefs, interpretive skills, personalities, and genius of the greatest musicians in the world, all brought together, allowing all of us with sensitivity and awareness to take advantage of musical knowledge and talent that few musicians have the opportunity to encounter.

This experience has been a tremendous help to me, not only as a performer, but even more so as a teacher. To be able to pass along to my students the superior musical ideas that I learned from the great masters is an important adjunct to what I teach from my own experience and experiments. How satisfying I find it to be able to say to a student, "This is the way pianist Artur Schnabel asked me to phrase the opening horn solo of the Brahms B♭ Piano Concerto," and then proceed to demonstrate it.

When I played the horn solo in *Till Eulenspiegel* our guest conductor, Karl Böhm, complimented me on playing it correctly. I explained that our regular conductor, Frederick Stock, had studied conducting and composition with Richard Strauss and Strauss had told him exactly how he wanted the horn solo played. Stock had explained to me how Strauss wanted it. Upon hearing this, Karl Böhm laughed and said, "No wonder you played it correctly! Stock and I were both students of Strauss at the same time and he explained the *Till* horn solo to both of us simultaneously."

I clearly remember the time in 1954 when our guest conductor, Georg Solti (now the music director of the Chicago Symphony), asked me for a certain beautiful nuance in the horn solo in Tchaikovsky's Fifth Symphony. I had never thought of it before, but because it was such a logical and beautiful bit of phrasing I always included it in subsequent performances. Conductors are always pleased by it, but perhaps they wouldn't be if they found out it was not my idea but that of a conductor of talent superior to theirs!

Gradually, through this exposure to grand music-making, I have formed ideas and formulas, as have most of my contemporaries, that enable me to teach in a more positive and meaningful manner. I can watch for problems and try to nip them in the bud, based on having already faced these same problems myself in the past, perhaps many times. I have evolved a formula of teaching, which came about mostly from these wonderful opportunities to work with the masters and learn something from each of them.

One thing that I have learned from this experience is that to succeed, a performer absolutely must have three important attributes. If any one of these attributes is missing the aspiring performer cannot possibly be successful. These attributes are:

The technique to do practically anything one wishes to do on the chosen instrument. This technique includes full range (high, low, and middle range, all with good tone), complete dynamic range (loud, soft), great facility (the ability to play fast and light, and also have superb control of slow passages), a beautiful singing tone, and impeccable intonation. Clean, clear staccato and a smooth, even legato are of great importance. All of this must be accomplished with superb accuracy.

Students often get the impression that the word technique refers to the ability to play passages at a breakneck speed, run scales up and down, make huge interval jumps and rapid arpeggios, and so on. Technique should and does encompass these abilities, but the word also means much more. The ability to hold a steady and beautiful tone and then make a smooth crescendo or diminuendo, arriving at the next point in the music at exactly the desired dynamic level — this, too, is part of technique. A clean staccato, a smooth legato, are part of a masterful technique, along with the ability to play very loud and very soft, with all the shadings in between. Technique certainly includes making intonation close to perfect, regardless of the fact that the music may be high or low, loud or soft, fast or slow. Technique involves deciding the best places to breathe or bow — the best fingerings to facilitate a passage. In general, technique is the ability to make your instrument do just about anything you wish it to do, regardless of whether or not that wish is musical or unmusical.

The musicianship to use this technique in an artistic and musically meaningful manner. This includes studying the phrasing and the style, telling a story (in the case of program music), observing the correct tempos, and giving careful consideration to dynamic levels, including crescendos and diminuendos. Musicianship is the musical projection of the thoughts and feelings of the composer and the performer.

Technique is needed to transform these musical ideas into vibrating airwaves, but it should always be subservient to musicianship. Use your technique to bring music to life, not to show off.

Musicianship can only be realized when the technique has become advanced enough that the performer can make the instrument behave in exactly the manner that his musicianship dictates. There is no point in having beautiful musical ideas if one cannot make the instrument reproduce these ideas as sounding airwaves.

Conversely, even the most astounding virtuosity is wasted if the performer does not have musically beautiful ideas to convey. So we must always keep in mind that technique without musicianship is worthless, just as is musicianship without technique.

Great technique is undoubtedly the result of years of hard work, notwithstanding the fact that natural aptitude plays a great part in success. Musicianship likewise takes great study, although good instincts are a priceless addition to this study. To develop these instincts, students need to realize that musicianship is simply good taste as applied to music.

In most cases good taste can be defined as moderation. Too much crescendo or diminuendo can be just as tasteless as no crescendo or diminuendo when the music calls for one of these nuances. Moderation is the solution of good taste. We have all heard someone play a virtuoso piece at a breakneck tempo, even though the speed is unmusical. Here we have a musician showing off at the expense of musicianship. On a few rare occasions moderation is not desirable. We want a violent storm in the *William Tell* Overture and wild abandon is suitable for the "Rapids" section of the *Moldau*. Most often though, moderation is the key to good musicianship.

Analysis is a necessary adjunct to musicianship. Study phrasing and look for the peak of the phrase so you can make the intensity of the music lead to that peak and then relax. This peak, or what I prefer to call the "pivot point" of a phrase, can come at the very beginning or the very end of the passage, but most often it will be found somewhere toward the middle of the phrase. It may take some thought to seek it out, but it is there somewhere in the phrase.

Simplify your articulation by remembering that any note you play can be started in only one of two ways. It can be articulated (we brass players refer to this as an "attack") or it can be slurred into from a previous note. Because there are only these two ways to start a note, by all means choose the right one. Well-written music will indicate this.

There are also only two ways to change your dynamic level — gradually (crescendo or diminuendo) or suddenly (subito). The music will tell you; choose the right one.

Determine what the tempo marking really means. Often the modifying adjective is a better clue to the tempo than is the major tempo indication. If, for instance, *allegro* means fast, isn't the composer trying to warn you not to play too fast when he writes *poco allegro*? Does not *molto vivace* mean extra fast? Watch those modifiers. They are your best warning as to what not to do. Pay attention to these words: *molto*; *meno*; *poco*; *assai*, and so on.

Analyze the title of the composition. All too often I find that the performer has not the foggiest notion of what the title means. The composer gave the composition a title because he was trying to illustrate that title with musical ideas. If you, as the performer, do not know what the title means, how can you honestly or adequately demonstrate the composer's musical ideas to the audience?

Here are a few random titles: *Polacca*; *Villanelle*; *Idyll*; *Allemande*; *Farandole*; *Elegy*. Do you know what they mean? Musicianship may come easily and instinctively to some fortunate individuals, but, like all other aspects of music, it can be learned, polished, and demonstrated by all of us.

The courage to present this technique and musicianship in public performance. Many would-be great performers have the requisite technique and musicianship but find that stage fright detracts so much from their level of performance that they cannot fully demonstrate these hard-earned skills in front of an audience. Somewhere during the study of musical performance this fear must be transformed into the courage to play before an audience with as much efficiency and musical quality as when playing in the practice studio. In fact, many seasoned performers build this ability to the point where they play even better when stimulated by a large audience.

Some may think that courage is too strong a word to indicate the kind of fortitude that is required when one steps out to play in front of an audience. Non-musicians find it difficult to believe that a musician will have even a touch of nervousness, let alone fear. After all, don't we "play" our instruments and isn't "play" something we do for enjoyment? The answer is yes, if we play an instrument only for recreation and have no really exacting standards. But when we are intensely serious about our playing to the point of making it our life's work — and source of income — we can feel performance pressures completely unknown to the dilettante.

A good example of the differing attitudes can be illustrated in this way: as an amateur "duffer" golfer I can laugh when I miss an easy putt. But the professionals at the major tournaments do not laugh when this happens to them. On the other hand, some of them, when playing a musical instrument for recreation, might laugh when they "fluff" an easy phrase. I do not laugh when I break a note!

Besides the nervousness resulting from simply facing an audience there can be other contributing factors. Obviously, nervousness and the need for courage are in direct proportion to the seriousness of the endeavor. There should be no surprise in finding oneself in need of courage when playing a difficult and important concert, perhaps in a major city with music critics and famous musicians in the audience.

In seeking the cure for nervousness and in gaining that needed courage it is well to analyze why one is nervous. Is it lack of practice? Nothing is more heartening than knowing that you can play the music, simply because you have done so dozens, or better yet, hundreds of times in recent practice sessions.

Are you nervous because you have not been on stage often enough? Then find every opportunity to get on the stage. Volunteer to play for school assemblies, church services, retirement homes, hospitals, shopping malls, social clubs, and so on. Nothing will give you more courage than to know that you can do it because you have done it many times before, "under fire." Find opportunities — make opportunities — to play in front of audiences. They needn't be critical audiences. The idea is to get used to that sea of faces!

Could the nervousness be the result of your conductor showing some recent displeasure at your performance? Then find out, by asking him, what he didn't like and how you might correct it. Might it be that after four years of hard work, you are about to play your senior recital? What a good reason to have played as many public performances as possible during those four years!

Could it be that the nervousness is induced by the fact that the rehearsals did not go well and now you wonder what hope there is for the concert? The answer is to be so well prepared, by preliminary practice, that even the rehearsals go well. Do not permit yourself to play poorly at rehearsals; this is very confidence shaking.

It is calming to realize that, important as a performance may be to you, it still is not an earth-shaking moment in that day's global events. You are not responsible for someone's life by being called on to perform a heart transplant or brain surgery. I don't say this to minimize the importance of the performance, but the realization that the sun will continue to rise and no one will be physically harmed, regardless of how your performance goes, can be the element that will allow you to perform with ease and confidence.

In your search for confidence on the stage be very conscientious not to resort to artificial aids: do not use stimulants or tranquilizers in order to do your life's work. Many musicians have sought to enhance their performance by habitually taking beta-blockers, alcohol, bromides, aspirin, marijuana, barbituates, or even steroids. How sad it is that someone would think it necessary to be enslaved by some artificial so-called aid in order to continue a lifetime endeavor.

A professional musician goes on the stage probably several times a week. Why not go about this daily work as naturally, honestly, and healthily as a businessman would go to his office? This is our chosen profession. Let us do our work in a natural, businesslike, and enthusiastic manner, without neuroses, hang-ups, or artificial aids. We musicians can and should be as normal and sensible as anyone else and with intelligence we too can enjoy long and happy careers.

It is the duty of the teacher to address all three of these aspects of performance with each student, varying the emphasis as appropriate. All teachers have had students who show superior technique but have poor musical taste; conversely, we have all had students who have lovely musical ideas but cannot express them because of their limited technical ability. Each student gets butterflies when he faces his first recital or difficult ensemble concert. Some of these students find this anticipation beneficial and will perform "over their heads" out of sheer heightened awareness. The large majority, though, will find that their nervousness or stage fright has a negative affect, causing them to play far below their practice room performance level.

The truth is that seldom does a teacher find a student who has all three of these aptitudes — technique, musicianship, and courage — in strong and equal proportions. When one does find such a pupil he will undoubtedly be working with a *wunderkind* — and they are rare, indeed. The happy fact is that the three attributes are all amenable to improvement. They can be brought up to acceptable or even superb performance levels by hard work, intelligent analysis, and the guidance of an experienced and sympathetic teacher or colleague.

I often think of myself in the role of teacher as a sort of glorified — or maybe not so glorified — tailor. Why a tailor? When I was in my late teens I went through a brief stage of physical growth when I could go into a men's clothing store and walk out with a certain size suit (if I remember correctly it was a 36 regular) and wear it home without the slightest alteration. The suit was a 36 regular and I was a 36 regular. Later, however, when I became a mature adult I started going to a tailor to get my suits. Why? I was no longer a perfect anything. A little overweight, a bit more stoop-shouldered than the perfect male, left arm ¼ inch longer than the right (lesson to be learned: switch hands occasionally when carrying your instrument case year after year!), I could no longer walk out of a store with a perfectly fitting suit because although the suit was perfect, I wasn't.

As a teacher I am in many ways like my old tailor. If there were such a thing as a perfect student he could go into a music store, buy one of the many fine method books available for his instrument, study it diligently, practice faithfully, and in due time become a full-fledged virtuoso. The method books, like the 36 regular suit, are designed for perfect human beings, who will, in their perfection, progress steadily and unswervingly without problems.

Because few perfect physical specimens or music students exist, both the tailor and the music teacher serve an important function. The tailor measures you, not only for your good points but also for your shortcomings. He then designs and builds a suit that is right for you and probably only you. Similarly the music teacher measures the student's abilities and weaknesses and designs lessons that fit these conditions, choosing or even composing exercises, etudes, and techniques, all designed to improve that individual student's musical ability. The teacher aims to make his students musically successful, just as the tailor strives to make his customers sartorially successful.

I will close with a quote from my book, *The Art of Musicianship*. This is probably my best description of what takes place in my own mind during a performance:

> Finally, in our search for control of nervousness in performance, I would be omitting a most important consideration if I did not include spiritual strength as a contributing factor. Call it faith, positive thinking, grace, belief, or what you will, the knowledge that you are not up there on the stage unguided and alone, has a very strengthening and calming effect.
>
> When I was a young man, twenty-two years of age, I suddenly found myself in the first horn position in the Chicago Symphony Orchestra, a responsibility for which I was not really ready, age-wise or experience-wise. I remember wondering, during many concerts, as a difficult solo approached inevitably closer, "What am I doing on this stage, at this moment, with this famous orchestra? What must I do now to be sure of 'getting' this solo? How do I set my lips? Should I breathe now or wait a moment longer? How does that fingering pattern go again? Why, oh why, did I ever accept this responsibility?" Somehow I survived this period of unrelieved negative thinking until the time came when I could rationalize in a more positive manner. And what a difference this made! Formerly, I had assumed that all the events leading up to my engagement by the Chicago Symphony were completely haphazard — a bit of luck here, a chance encounter there, until I eventually ended up in the Chicago Symphony, as unpredictable as a seashell washes up on a beach. But, with my change in thinking came the realization that perhaps all these apparently haphazard events weren't haphazard at all. Perhaps, back in high school, when I had that fight with the gym teacher, and the supervisor suggested that I could fill my physical education requirement by switching to the marching band, it was not just an aimless suggestion. Was it mere chance that the street car conductor, after telling me I could no longer bring my beloved tuba on board because it blocked traffic, pointed to a French horn being carried by another bandsman, and told me that I would be allowed to bring "one of them" on board? Was it fate that made me take his advice? Suppose he had pointed to a clarinet or a violin? Would I now be a clarinetist or a violinist? The more I pondered these questions the more convinced I became that it wasn't all just haphazard — that I wasn't just a seashell washed up willy-nilly on the Chicago Symphony's shore. So it wasn't just a series of unrelated, random events which eventually put me on that stage. It was a series of incredibly interwoven and predestined events which put me there. Whether you, the reader, choose not to believe in this way or whether I have made an entirely erroneous analysis of my progress, is beside the point. The important thing is that I no longer felt that I was on that stage "accidentally," powerless to know whether I would play well or badly. Now I *knew* that I was there "on purpose." I was there because I had been led there by an amazing chain of events, not just mere coincidence, and

because I had been led there, certainly I could do the work assigned to me. I was now there because it was planned for me, and failure was not part of that plan.

One can argue that it was this new positive attitude which gave me the courage to play confidently and well, and not because of some celestial plan for me. Or one can claim that it was this celestial plan that gave me the positive attitude. In either case, one fact remains: believing that you are playing on the stage at that moment because you are capable of doing it will result in a better performance. Was it because a Supreme Being helped you or was it only because you believed in a Supreme Being? Perhaps you will never know. But you will know that something helped you!

The Farkas studio, a log cabin built in 1855

On Horn Playing
An interview with James H. Winter

When in Chicago last month for the Midwest Band Clinic, I had the pleasure of a quiet talk with Philip Farkas, with whom, I am proud to say, have studied with at various times. Inevitably, we talked about horns and horn players (I suppose horn players do actually talk about other things, too), and so much of what he said seemed to me to be of interest to the readers of this magazine that I asked his permission to report as much as I could remember, and he agreed. Here are what I feel to be the more pertinent gleanings:

About converting trumpet or cornet players to horn: Above all, convert the better players, not those who simply aren't making the grade. The usual reason for changing a student over to horn from cornet or trumpet (and why is it that they almost never convert the other direction?) is an excess of cornets and trumpets and a shortage of hornists. Reluctant to lose the better lead players in the band, the director is all too likely to make his switch from the back of the cornet section, with the result that he still doesn't have a horn section.

By all means, work on the students who give evidence of at least a reasonable musical talent and who have made a good start on their first instrument, thereby indicating perseverence and desire. If possible, further selection can be made by taking the players who, although otherwise capable, tend to play with an excessively dark, almost fuzzy, tone; there is every chance that such a student is by nature a horn player who simply happened to start on another instrument. And when you have started the conversion process, be sure to warn the convert he must plan to practice at least twice as much as he did before!

With regard to the embouchure, certain concepts must be changed. To begin with, many trumpet players place the mouthpiece pretty well down on the lower lip; this must be changed at once, with the mouthpiece being moved well onto the upper lip. It will be well also to place emphasis almost entirely on the low register for two reasons: the first is the obvious one that the low register will probably give the most difficulty by the very nature of the change; the second is that this emphasis on the low tones will

This article is reprinted from the April 1959 issue of *Woodwind World* help to open and relax the embouchure, and to get away from the characteristically tenser trumpet embouchure.

Conversely, most trumpet players tend to play with the lower jaw slightly extended; this should *not* be changed. The student may tend to pull his jaw back too far, resulting in an overbite, because of the other changes he is making. The horn embouchure requires just as firm and flat a plane as any other. Also, the slightly extended jaw helps to give the player an appropriately aggressive look, which is important in establishing proper relationships with conductors!

Most trumpet and cornet students use a definite *ta* attack, which will be found much too explosive for the horn; the long, tenuous air column of the horn will not tolerate anything more explosive than a *da*. It will take a while for the student to gain confidence that this is sufficient, but in fact, his chances for accuracy will be greatly enhanced if he avoids trying to force the horn to speak. Conversely, he must not be allowed to use a gooey, pushed attack; the tone must speak immediately.

In addition to all this, of course, the right hand will have to be watched for a while, and the whole conception of tone production will have to be reorganized in terms of a true horn sound.

Less technical reminiscences and suggestions to the young player: Most conductors, while they will not tolerate slovenly playing, are tolerant of the occasional slip which is almost an inevitable part of the hornist's life. Such tolerance is, of course, a boost to the player and helps him to play more musically. For example, George Szell once advised Mr. Farkas, "Don't ever become a *careful* player, I am more interested in what you do with the notes you get than in how many you miss." On an earlier occasion, Karl Krueger (then in Kansas City, where Mr. Farkas began his professional career) reported that he had been waylaid by an elderly gentleman after a concert; the old fellow said he had enjoyed the concert well enough, but that Mr. Krueger's first horn had missed a note. Krueger looked him straight in the eye and solemnly said, "My! What a terrific ear you have."

Apropos of all this, European orchestras generally seem more relaxed than U.S. groups, and the continental and English players in consequence seem to enjoy their playing more than our people do. Since the advent of the tape recorder, recording sessions are actually easier on the nerves than live performances; in the old days, recording was downright agony, because the slightest slip required recutting a whole twelve-inch disc, whereas with present techniques, the offending measure or two can be replayed and then edited into place. In the disc days, each passing second of the three and a half to four minutes required for a side was accompanied by a rise in tension in almost geometric ratio, so that the careful listener could literally hear a long solo passage changing from an artistic expression to desperate note-grabbing.

On the other hand, the relative ease with which flawless recordings can be produced has accustomed the concert-goer to perfection, so that the live performance is perhaps now more taxing for the orchestra personnel than it used to be.

Regarding the young player with professional aspirations — most of them simply have no concept of the demands which will be made upon them by a major professional orchestra, and they undergo a rude awakening during their first couple of seasons. Probably the biggest failing of the novice is his lack of dynamic range; he has never been forced to play the excruciating *pianissimo* which is expected as a matter of course by the professional conductor; and curiously enough, he also is most unlikely to be able to hold his own in a professional brass section playing *fortissimo*. He is also dismayed to find that his solo quality, which projected so easily in the Tchaikowsky Fifth over perhaps fifteen to thirty strings of student quality, simply doesn't get off the stage when it must sound through a full section of mature players using fine string instruments. He has also the great problem of knowing, or sensing, when his part, regardless of the printed dynamics, must either project or be submerged into the ensemble.

Eric Delamarter once summarized the three stages of the professional musician thus: The novice is likely to be good, in his very naivete; he simply hasn't found out yet how hard it really is and hasn't developed nerves. In the second stage, he has a sobering realization of the problems ahead and acquires plenty of nerves! If he survives this critical stage, he becomes a true professional; he never fully conquers his preconcert jitters and he is fully aware of the hazards confronting him, but he has learned to cope both with himself and with the external factors. He has become a real trouper who simply doesn't allow himself a bad day and can be depended upon to produce every time. At this stage, his value to an orchestra cannot be overestimated.

Eight Fundamentals Hold Key to Success
by Philip Farkas

If good horn playing consisted of playing capably a mezzoforte in the middle register, the world would have literally thousands of good hornists. Unfortunately, or perhaps I should say fortunately, one's playing is judged by his ability in the difficult registers and dynamics.

The comparatively few fine French horn artists who have "everything" have learned either consciously or unconsciously to concentrate on mastering the "extremes." By this I mean the extreme high or low registers, the extreme fortissimo or pianissimo, extremely fast velocity, or extremely slow, sustained legato. And all these extremes in all the possible combinations!

These artists practice not only the pleasant middle registers, dynamics, and tempos, but also spend many hours a week perfecting the fatiguing high and low registers, both pianissimo and fortissimo.

They learn their fast passages faster than necessary in order to have that essential margin of safety when playing under the stress of a concert. They practice their slow, sustained solos even slower to develop breath control and an unhurried singing, sostenuto. In short, the successful hornist practices his "extremes."

There are really very few fundamentals in horn playing, perhaps just eight. All the more reason then that each of these important fundamentals become habit. These fundamentals are:

1. A beautiful characteristic horn tone; 2. a smooth, controlled legato; 3. a sharp, clean staccato; 4. a clear, free range of at least three octaves; 5. a solid fortissimo through entire range; 6. a clear, controlled pianissimo through entire range; 7. a steady crescendo and diminuendo, and 8. good velocity in all scales and arpeggios.

Only eight fundamentals — but they cover all the technical needs of the hornist! However, none of them are easy to master. The final conquering of them comes only after many hours of painstaking labor. When they are finally under control and can be properly combined at will, they will enable the performer to negotiate the most formidable passages.

Musicianship is the most vital fundamental of all. It is a wonderful gift to come by naturally, but to those not so gifted a great deal can be acquired by intelligent thought and logic.

Taken from the 1957 Winter Edition of *Meyer's Band News*

Musicianship simply stated, is good taste in music, and musical taste is merely a matter of knowing, or doing, things in moderation, neither too little nor too much; a little finesse when called for, boldness in the proper place, and always uppermost, the playing of music, not notes.

To musicianship should be added the musicians' consciousness of his particular instrument's characteristic qualities. The horn's outstanding characteristic is its beautiful, mystical tone. It should be smooth, slightly veiled, yet clear, with its typical slight tinge of brassiness in the louder passages.

The very smooth legato, almost portamento in effect, is another characteristic quality which the player should have the ability to bring out when needed. The horn's ability to make beautiful and dramatic crescendi and diminuendi are often tellingly used by symphonic composers. Church bell effects and the ominous buzz of the hand stopped notes are frequently used.

All these qualities are so characteristic of the horn that the player must strive to develop them to the utmost in order to bring out its full individuality. The performer must not only be a musician but an ardent student of the horn, working always to develop the full beauty and characteristic style inherent in this poetic instrument.

Phil and his Airplane, a 1949 225 Navion

Excerpts from
The Art of French Horn Playing

The horn is just like the horn on the old-fashioned phonograph, an amplifier. It magnifies the vibration of the lips at the same time vibrating in sympathy with them and adding its own tonal characteristics. (page 19)

Since, therefore, there is always mouthpiece pressure to a certain extent, it is important to distribute it evenly on the entire contact surface of the lips. Even very mild pressure might conceivably become unbearable if concentrated on one small spot of the embouchure. It is exactly this same theory of weight distribution that allows a person to successfully effect a rescue on thin ice by crawling on his stomach where a moment before the victim's weight, being concentrated on the soles of his shoes, caused him to crash through. (page 26)

The resistance in the lip should be just enough to produce vibration, but the feeling is that of air escaping through the lips with *almost* no impedance. (page 27)

When playing loud, let the embouchure take it easy and depend on the air to do the work. (page 28)

Get into the habit of practicing extremes. (page 45)

Whatever the difficulty, it is the player's duty to discover and conquer it *to the extreme*. Is the passage very fast? Then, little by little, learn to play it faster than it will ever be needed. Having technique to spare will pay dividends under the stress of actual performance. This extreme approach can be used on all problems with very gratifying results. (page 45)

I have heard this amazing plan all too often when questioning pupils: "I couldn't practice every day this week, but I kept up my three hour average by practicing six hours every other day!" This plan and its many variations will work no better than the plan I once made as a child to eat all three meals of the day at breakfast time and thus be free to play all day without the bother of stopping to eat. (page 46)

Some players feel that because they have "observed the letter of the law" and avoided attacking a note, they have successfully made a slur. However, the slur must not only be done right mechanically, but must also *sound* right musically. (page 47)

The word "attack" is misleading, as it infers a thrust forward. (page 49)

One of the most common faults is the method of tonguing *forward* and *backward* into the lip opening. (page 49)

Keep the main body of the tongue motionless and well down in the bottom of the mouth. Then curl the tip of it upward until it resembles the point on a ski. The tongue is now in a position to be helped in its attack by the air, which will tend to push it in a downward direction. (page 49)

For all other effects of tonguing, this air seal is broken more or less gently. It is for these different effects that we articulate a hard *too* or soft *too* or the varying degree of *doo*. Each of these articulations breaks the air seal in a different manner to achieve the desired effect. Let us bear in mind that the tongue's principal function in these various attacks is to give a clean, musical start to the vibration of the lips. (page 50)

A word of caution: *never* stop the air column abruptly by using the tongue, as in forming the articulation *toot*. Simply stop all air pressure immediately, at the moment the note is to stop. Perhaps the most accurate description of the articulation would be the syllable *tooh* or *tuh*. (page 51)

Therefore, avoid becoming the loudest or softest, highest or lowest, brightest or darkest player in the world. Become, if possible, the horn player who best exemplifies all the desirable characteristics of the instrument. This is particularly important in regard to tone. Too dark, too bright, too open, too closed, too brassy, too smooth; any one of these extremes might be the cause of an unnatural tone. Strive for the most beautiful, natural, characteristic tone possible. (page 52)

When and if you find a player who has everything (according to your taste), don't be afraid to emulate him. You will not be an imitator. The very fact that you admire him shows that you have similar musical tastes, and you have a great advantage in having them crystallized for you by an artist. (page 52)

Tone quality can be only as healthy as the air-column which supports it. (page 53)

I think it would be preferable to concentrate on the *direct result* of its proper use rather than on the diaphragm itself. That is, concentrate on filling the horn with air. In other words, "follow through" with the air. Blow *through* the horn, not *at* it. Develop the tone by getting the feeling that you are expanding it. (page 53)

So let us not forget, in our striving for technical proficiency, that unless all this acquired technique is used to produce *musical* music, it has been learned in vain. (page 54)

Finally, but very important to the success of obtaining high notes easily, there is the knack of lipping the notes up or down with almost a "flick" of the lip. (page 58)

Good endurance is one of the most reliable proofs of correct playing methods. (page 62)

There will be no doubt in one's mind when it is just right, as the softest *pianissimo* will then seem to float out of the horn without effort. (page 64)

Strive to develop the clear, pure *pianissimo* which has real tone but little volume. (page 64)

I should remark at this point that a really fine *pianissimo* is the scarcest quality among brass players. (page 64)

A slightly sharp instrument played with a relaxed embouchure, to bring it down to exact pitch, will always have a more beautiful, singing tone than a flat instrument lipped up. Endurance will also be greatly increased. (page 82)

Horn players are very careful not to punish their embouchures on the day of an important concert, which is, of course, sensible. But they often "cram" their practice on the day before such a concert, reasoning that it is their last opportunity. From observation, I believe that this is almost as detrimental as abusing the lip on the very day of the performance. There is a tendency for the lips to get stiff and insensitive the day following a strenuous workout. Observe your own tendencies and note whether or not this is true in your own case. If so, try practicing heavily *two* days before the concert, then pamper the lip carefully one day before the performance. The result should be a very flexible, responsive embouchure when you want it — the day of the concert. (page 83)

Stage-fright. This is a common ailment, and it might be a comfort just to know that almost every musician, including our world-famous soloists, have experienced it at some time or another. (page 83)

When kept under control, nervousness can become an asset to the performer, as it sharpens the senses and often inspires one to "play over his own head." (page 83)

Most stage-fright comes from the novelty of facing an audience too infrequently. (page 84)

You are not about to perform an operation in which someone's life will be at stake! You are simply going to make some music and make it as beautifully as possible. (page 84)

Take several deep breaths before starting a performance, whenever the occasion permits. (page 84)

Excerpts from
The Art of Brass Playing

The muscular feeling while playing throughout the instrument's range is one of varying degrees of tension and relaxation *but not one of lip motion* or commotion. (page 15)

Any embouchure shape will speak if we blast enough air through it. Therefore we must pay a great deal more attention to the ability to play softly and delicately when determining the quality of our own or a student's embouchure. (page 38)

One of the finest exercises advocated by many of the older German brass instructors is the practicing of attacks without aid from the tongue. More frequent use of this exercise would clear up many of our so-called tonguing problems. (page 45)

The lightest touch of the tongue would now be sufficient for a clean attack because the instrument and lips are vibrating in sympathy. In fact, it is almost impossible to produce a bad attack with even the most haphazard type of tonguing. Try it! (page 45)

A broken note is just a note that is *too far* out of tune; and a beautiful tone can only result from well-centered placement of pitch on each note. (page 46)

The object of buzzing the mouthpiece is to produce a good "rich" buzz, and one which is *exactly* in tune. In fact, *if you can't play it on the mouthpiece, you can't play it on the instrument. (page 46)*

Staccato does *not* mean as short as possible, but only relatively shorter than the normal value of the note. There are many passages in Beethoven's music, for example, where we find a *staccato* mark (a dot) over half-notes in a slow passage. (page 47)

Too often the misguided player attempts to get shortness in his *staccato* notes by stopping the vibration with the tongue — "tut tut tut." This abrupt stopping of the air-column, and its consequent abrupt stoppage of the tone, produces a most unmusical and unnatural quality. No *musical* instrument in the world stops its sound suddenly. All of them, including xylophone and *pizzicato* violin, invariably produce tones with tapered endings. In other words, any *musical* note, no matter how short, has a *diminuendo* at its very end. (page 47)

Certainly proper and copious *inhalation* must precede successful blowing. Obviously, if the player does not first inhale a generous quantity of air, he cannot, a moment later, project a large, sustained air-column. Childish as such an observation may seem, it is at this point in the breathing cycle that the student frequently fails. (page 59)

The great number of foregoing pages might lead you to believe that brass playing is extremely difficult, or at least lead you to believe that I think it is! Such is not the case. I believe brass playing is quite natural an act, an almost instinctive one. (page 65)

When one has this instinct for brass playing, he needs but two other attributes to make his playing successful — moderately normal teeth, lips and general physique, and a feeling for music, so that when the physical control is gained, that which comes out of the horn-bell is worth hearing. Did I say two attributes? There is that third one, willingness to practice! Without this one, all the others are completely worthless. But, having these attributes, make use of them, and the final result will profoundly enhance and enrich your life. (page 65)

Therefore, pursue your brass playing with enthusiasm, and let the results take you where they will. This much I can guarantee: Mastering your horn will repay your efforts many times over, and this inanimate brass object will then take on an entity and personality, which like any other true friend, can enrich and vitalize your entire life. (page 65)

Excerpts from
The Art of Musicianship

Generally, good taste results in moderation, although there are musical expressions of a violent type which might require violent excesses and those of a purposely monotonous nature which would call for an underplayed, humdrum effect. (page 7)

"Relative" is the catchword in a study of dynamics. No dynamic is limited to only one exact volume. (page 13)

One could make a quite accurate blanket statement by claiming that most music students do not play soft enough in *pp* nor loud enough for *ff*. (page 15)

I sincerely believe that there is no rhythm deficiency in any musician which cannot be remedied by a careful and intelligent study of subdivision. (page 22)

Regardless of its simplicity or difficulty, every passage has to become a tune before we can play it in tune. (page 38)

When, finally, that perfect run-through is accomplished, then, and only then, is the performer ready to start *practice* of that passage. (page 48)

Not only does this *repetitive* type of practice build confidence, it *programs the computer*. (page 48)

Finally, in our search for control of nervousness in performance, I would be omitting a most important consideration if I did not include spiritual strength as a contributing factor. Call it faith, positive thinking, grace, belief, or what you will, the knowledge that you are not up there on the stage unguided and alone, has a very strengthening and calming effect. (page 50)

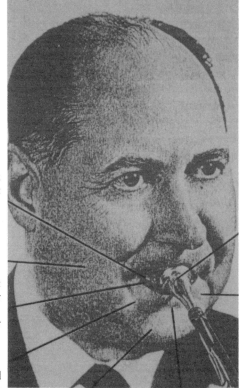

Lips are puckered, cheek muscles are not stretching lips.

Cheeks have tension, as though smiling.

Lower lip is not tucked-in nor swallowed behind upper lip.

"U" shaped valley formed by muscle tension.

Mouthpiece correctly placed on the lips in its up-down position, according to the instrument being played.

Jaw is not clenched shut, but is held quite open, teeth well apart.

Instrument kept quite horizontal.

Lower jaw is thrust forward so that lower front teeth align with upper front teeth.

Chin arched down. No horizontal wrinkle.

Embouchure components which combine to form "the brass players face."

136

For many years now, just before going out to perform, I have read a little page taken from a booklet, *Creative Thought for Each Day* (published by Religious Science International, 885 East Telegraph Road, Fillmore, California 93015) which I have found to be inspiring and confidence-building. In the sincere hope that it will offend no one and that it might help others as it has helped me, I am placing this page at the very end of the book. In that way, if it offends your beliefs, you may tear it out and destroy it without defacing the book. If you feel neutral about it you may let it remain and ignore it. But, if you believe as I do, that it is inspiring, cut it out and keep it in your music case so that you can read it just before going on stage. It will reaffirm why you are here, what your abilities are, and why yours is an exalted work. (page 50)

I Am In My Right Place

"The Lord will perfect that which concerneth me . . ."
—Psalm 138:8.

I am now the person God intended me to be. I am now fulfilling my divine destiny in perfect ways under grace. I am here where the One has placed me, doing what He has given me to do, in the way He has shown me to do it. When it needs to be done in new ways, He will prompt me to do it His way. All results are in His hand, therefore, I will rejoice in what I do and bless the way it is done.

God, Who loves and appreciates me as His own expression, is everywhere evenly present, approving the work He is doing by means of me, for He has placed Himself at the center of every man's being. He is over all His works and whatsoever He doeth is perfect. Nothing can be added to it and nothing can be taken from it, for God doeth it. He will instruct me and teach me in the way I shall go; He will guide me with His eye.

Anita Scofield

The Amazing Philip Farkas
by Louis Davidson
Professor Emeritus of Music, Indiana University

In attempting to enumerate the many remarkable gifts and qualities of the likes of Philip Farkas where does one begin? This is not an easy task, for while the one thing that comes most readily to mind is his outstanding qualities as a performer he has also excelled in a number of other areas tangential to music. Consider the variety and range of his achievements:

Performer

One must begin with Philip Farkas the performer. Is there anyone, anywhere, who has ever heard him play who did not thrill to the beauty of his sound, to his superb musicianship and overall artistry? He was ever, and still remains, the artist supreme, the artist extraordinary. His musical background and the wealth of his experience as an orchestral player are most formidable. To wit: (at age 19) Kansas City Philharmonic (Karl Krueger) 1933-36; Chicago Symphony (Frederick Stock) 1936-41; Cleveland Symphony (Artur Rodzinski) 1941-45; Boston Symphony Orchestra (Serge Koussevitsky) 1945-46; Cleveland Symphony — 2nd time (George Szell) 1946-47; Chicago Symphony — 2nd time (Rodzinski, Kubelik, Reiner) 1947-60; Aspen Music Festival (as teacher and performer) 1960-76.

In all the above he was always performing, of course, as solo horn. In 1960, he resigned from the Chicago Symphony to join the faculty of the School of Music of Indiana University as a full professor and has remained in that position up to the present.

This is truly an enviable record and a difficult one to match. One can be sure that Phil gave of himself unstintingly at all times and under all conditions. He has always had the respect and admiration, not only of his colleagues and peers, but also of every conductor with whom he has ever played, and he has played with the greatest of them. If there is such a thing as perfection, that elusive goal we all constantly strive for and very rarely achieve, it can truly be said of Phil's performances over these decades that he came as close to the realization of it as anyone possibly could.

Phil has recorded one solo album titled *Philip Farkas French Horn Solos*. It is on the Coronet recording label, Stereo #1293-S. He constantly threatens to make other records but procrastinates endlessly by rationalizing that, "Maybe next year I'll play better." One can't help but wonder how he can possibly "play better next year" in view of the fact that he has been playing so marvelously well right along.

Teacher

While in recent years the phrase "a legend in his own time" has become an overworked cliche and somewhat frazzled by its abuse and misuse, still, in its purest sense it remains the one phrase most appropriate to Phil Farkas because it applies to him on so many levels.

Past and present, his students are legion. Among them are several principal horn players in major symphony orchestras. Indeed, as a measure of his success it is safe to say that there are few symphony orchestras in America (and some in Europe) whose horn sections do not count among their members at least one, if not more, former Farkas students. However, not all of his students chose to pursue orchestral careers. Many of them were attracted to the field of education and have since become highly successful as teachers (as well as performers) in a large number of colleges and universities throughout the United States and Canada.

By the example of their own devotion to music and their successes either as orchestral players or teachers, these former students continue to perpetuate the Farkas tradition of forever aiming one's sights at the highest performing and musical standards of excellence possible. These are the goals Philip Farkas set for himself from the very beginning. Needless to say, he achieved an extraordinary realization of those goals.

Reflecting on the tremendous success he has had as a teacher over a span of more than forty years, it would not be amiss to say of him that he is truly "A Teacher's Teacher."

Author

Among other things for which Phil Farkas is famed the world over are the four preeminently successful books he has authored. They are: *The Art of French Horn Playing* (1956), *The Art of Brass Playing* (1962), *A Photographic Study of 40 Virtuoso Horn Players' Embouchures* (1970), and *The Art of Musicianship*(1976).

It is doubtful that there remains a French horn player here in America (or elsewhere) who has not heard of or who has not read

The Art of French Horn Playing. As for *The Art of Brass Playing*, are there any brass players left anywhere who are not acquainted with or who have not read it? About the four books, it can be stated that each is the definitive work on the subject with which it deals. Each has made a major contribution to the world of brass playing. As for his most recent book, *The Art of Musicianship*, it serves as an invaluable source of guidance and information not only to brass players but to all musicians.

In the last few years there has been a Japanese edition of *The Art of Brass Playing*. In the near future there will also be a French, a German and a Hungarian edition of this book (another testament to its importance and worth).

The Farkas Model Holton French Horn

For some time Phil Farkas had been thinking of a number of things that could be done to improve the French horn. He owned seven of them of various makes. Each of them had some excellent qualities which, however, were offset by a variety of negative qualities. He kept thinking of how he could incorporate all the good features of his seven horns into one horn and eliminate all of the bad features. Being of a mechanical turn of mind, Phil had definite ideas on how this could be done. What he needed above all was an instrument manufacturer who had all the mechanical and technological facilities for realizing this dream horn and, equally important, would be interested in embarking on, and financially supporting, such a project.

Success did not come overnight. There were many months of experimentation, of changes in the original design, certain innovations and periods of trial and error and frustration. But with each step in the evolution of the new model there was always an improvement over the previous work in progress. Then came the day after much grueling, arduous labor that Phil's dream of the perfect horn became a reality. It was no longer a dream; it was a fact. And what better, more appropriate name could that horn have than (what else?) The Holton Farkas Model French Horn.

Its success has been phenomenal. It is probably the best selling French horn in America today. But not only has the Farkas model horn received such wide acceptance here in America, but on a five week tour of Europe in the fall of 1979, Phil was tremendously pleased to find that a large number of European horn players were playing his horn. Particularly gratifying to him was the fact that in Germany, the birthplace of so many makes of fine French horns, a number of horn players there were playing Holton Farkas Model horns.

However, giving credit where credit is due, it must be said that the ever-increasing popularity of the Holton Farkas Model French Horn can in large measure be laid at the door of Vito Pascucci. This man of great vision provided dynamic leadership as president of the Leblanc/Holton Company. Thanks to him, the instrument has been given great visibility and name recognition via a brilliant advertising campaign.

Honors

In recent years a number of well-earned and richly-deserved honors have been bestowed upon Phil Farkas in recognition of his extraordinary qualities and achievements, both as a musician and as a human being.

They include:

1972 (and again in 1980) Host of the International Horn Workshop;

1975 Judge at the International Horn Competition in Munich, West Germany;

1978 Honorary Doctor of Music degree from Eastern Michigan University;

1979 The title of Distinguished Professor of Music was conferred upon him by Indiana University. It is the most prestigious of all I.U. titles.

1981 At this year's New York Brass Conference for Scholarships he is being honored by his peers and colleagues with a "Salute to Phil Farkas." This marks the first time since its inception in 1972 that the Brass Conference has given its salute to a French horn player.

Phil also holds honorary memberships in two musical fraternities — Kappa Kappa Psi and Phi Mu Alpha Sinfonia.

New York Brass Conference for Scholarships
March, 1981

141

Phil Farkas and His Horn Heard 'Round the World

by Nick Matavuli

If Phil Farkas, 68, would blow his French horn from his terrace on the highest hill, the pure sound would be heard on the other side of the hill, as the raw sound of a horn, a bull's horn, was heard across the wall of Jericho, over two millenia ago. Farkas is living in the country, compliments of the history of his favorite instrument.

"I still get goose-pimples before I play; there is the evolution of history in those notes," he noted. They were first heard before Christ was born. The purity of his notes is the result of a quarter-century of playing for the world's leading symphony orchestras on a French horn he designed himself. When he makes music, unintentionally, he's blowing the horn for America, for he was born in Chicago, the heart of America, and was musically educated in this country. You don't have to be a Parisian to excel in the French horn, after all.

His major musical publications have been translated for the world's benefit in several foreign languanges, including French. Professor Farkas has been teaching the art of playing the French horn at Indiana University since 1960, recently retiring with the title of distinguished professor. The word "distinguished" means more than an honorary title. It's awarded to a privileged few, the "non plus ultras" in their field. It takes sacrifice and hard work to get there, though.

"When you are a musician in a symphony orchestra, you are doomed to live in a big city," he said. "It's practicing downtown every morning and playing a concert every night. Before we were married, I warned my wife, Peg, 'We must go where the horn takes us,' and she went along with it," he said. The horn took the Chicagoan to the Kansas City Philharmonic, under the direction of Karl Krueger, and later George Szell; to the Cleveland Orchestra, under Artur Rodzinski; to the Boston Symphony, under Serge Koussevitsky, and, of course, to the Chicago Symphony Orchestra where he started playing and where he ended his symphonic journey in 1960, being last conducted by the legendary Fritz Reiner. Reiner would not have traded his native first horn for any European counterpart.

This article is taken from the January 1983 Bloomington *Herald*.

"When we arrived in Bloomington 22 years ago, we moved to the country, and there we offered our four daughters (Carol, Lynn, Jean and Margaret) a permanent home, although a little late in life," observed the father. "They would not move from Bloomington under any circumstances," he observed.

The Farkas' home is more than a terrestrial domicile. It's a Garden of Eden, with a terrace overlooking the earth down below, and the swimming pool springing from rocks. Birds, doves, squirrels and chipmunks are knocking on the door when the lady of the house is a minute late feeding them, and when her husband doesn't blow his horn at the regular time.

"We never suffer from isolation, with our four daughters and their husbands frequently visiting us, bringing along our grandchildren," the family man rejoiced.

Farkas is also a pilot. "When we need a change of pace, we board our own airplane and take off for Florida," he smiled. They took off right after this interview.

The famous horn player took me to a log house by the main house, dating back to Indian times. There shine all the mementos of his illustrious career, hardly based on a traditional, musical family history. "My grandfather was a breeder of the famous Husar horses in Budapest, which he planned to take to America and continue raising them there," he recounted, "but the cattle ship with the horses sank in the middle of the ocean, and, sadly enough, he spent the rest of his life working in a factory in Cleveland." His father had better luck. "Although my Dad was born in Budapest, he moved to Vienna at age four, then four years later, came to America; he graduated from Purdue and set up an advertising agency in Chicago with his brother, Frank," recounted the son.

"As to my musical career, I started in a Boy Scout Camp where they needed a bugler, and I volunteered to become one," chuckled the master. At the time he was only 11 years old. Previously, he had taken piano lessons, but hated it.

"It so happened that I could not get the right sound from the bugle, until a college student, a jazz trumpet player, showed me how to buzz my lips," he said. Today, musicians the world over, come to Professor Farkas with similar problems, only of a greater magnitude, so delicate they could ruin their professional career. "A Dutch musician, playing for the Amsterdam Symphony Orchestra, flew here to consult me on a lip problem he had, which I corrected, and am glad to say, he's still playing for the same orchestra," revealed the teacher. "Sometimes, I'm more like a doctor than a musician."

But when the "doctor" had a problem of his own as a youth, a "loud" one, he had to drop his bugle and grab a tuba, like it or not. It was a harsh change, indeed.

"By now I was in junior high school, Hirsch Junior High, and one day I yelled in the swimming pool during a gym class, loud enough that the physical education teacher got mad and threw his whistle at me that left a bruise," he recalled. His father would not stand for it, and requested his son's withdrawal from gym activity, which was substituted with a place in the marching band. " 'We have one opening for a drummer and one for a tuba player; which one will it be?' they asked me," he recalled. He took the tuba, only to find out, after six months, that it was too big to be carried back and forth to school on the streetcar. "The streetcar operator put a stop to it, pointing at a French horn a student was carrying on the streetcar. 'How about taking up something like that?' he suggested."

And "something like that" he took, which, after his high school graduation landed him a job as first horn with the Chicago Symphony Orchestra.

"There is a tremendous turnover among principal horn-players, because you play solo; one mistake and you are out," the perennial survivor pointed out. He cashed in on it. "It was one of the highest-paying positions in the orchestra," he acknowledged.

It's evident that he did more than survive in his native city. He got united by pure chance with a singer, a beautiful Texan, with whom he since has made "beautiful music" for 43 years.

"In addition to playing for the Chicago Orchestra, I was teaching at Chicago's Musical College and dating some of the students," he grinned. "Peg was studying voice at the same college, but I was dating another girl, who, that particular evening, was late for a date, so I improvised and asked Peg out," he smiled. Immediately the two harmonized and let the wedding bells ring. "Have horn, will travel," they let it be known, to Cleveland, Kansas City, Boston, Europe, anywhere! So Phil Farkas' symphonic journey began. It was indeed a sentimental journey: a Texas girl on his left side; his French horn, his first love, on his right side. He loves them both, in different ways.

144

"I didn't travel very much with my main orchestras, but I went to Europe several times with other symphony orchestras, recently touring the continent with the New Orleans Symphony Orchestra, and all along, with the Woodwind Quintet," he said.

Luckily for him, he was active in the Chamber Music Quintet, parallel to his main job, several years before coming to Bloomington. "When Dean Bain offered me the job to teach at I.U. I could not have adjusted to the new teaching position were it not for the American Woodwind Quintet here, which I joined and which made up for the loss of my musical fraternity in the big orchestra, my fellow musicians sitting side by side with me for years and sharing the same problems all musicians have," he said. "Believe me, it's a very closely knit family."

Gradually, the loss became a beautiful memory for the maestro, and the new challenge of teaching the French horn replaced performing with it. Soon he turned into a Szell or a Reiner of the classroom instead of the podium, and passed on his expertise to the young talents from the four corners of the world.

When he occasionally misses one of those "musical corners," due to semi-retirement, he hops in his plane and flies there and toots his horn to the delight of the sophisticated audiences. To think that, were it not for a rude gym teacher and a streetcar driver, he would have bugled somewhere in the woods instead, and the world would not have learned that America is capable of producing a French horn virtuoso.

Professor Ends Illustrious Career
by Julie Peterson

Philip Farkas will show you his former studio with more than a little pride; the grand piano that he had for 22 years, the places where the pictures used to hang.

Farkas, one of only four I.U. Distinguished Professors of Music and a world-renowned French horn player, is retiring from the University at age 68, after 22 years of teaching.

"It's hard to move out," Farkas said. "Each picture you take down has a certain memory to it. It gets you a little."

Farkas says he got into music indirectly. "I had no plans ever to be a musician. You drift into it; I went in the back door."

Farkas joined the marching band in junior high as a substitute for gym, which his parents wouldn't let him take. He used to carry his instrument, a tuba, on the street car every day.

"After about six months of this," he said, "the conductor told me I couldn't bring it on board any more because I was blocking traffic. I asked him what he would let me bring, and he pointed to a kid with a French horn and said, 'one of them.' So I went out and rented 'one of them.' If he had pointed to a flute, I would have gone out and rented a flute."

Whether or not he planned it, Farkas loved the horn and devoted a lot of time to it. At 18, he left high school to become the first horn with the Kansas City Philharmonic Orchestra.

"At the time, I didn't realize it was exceptional," Farkas said. "However, I think the standards were lower then. In those days, if you owned a horn and knew which end to blow in, you were already halfway in, because it was such a rare instrument."

After performing in Kansas City, Farkas took a number of orchestra jobs in rapid succession. He became first horn with the Chicago Symphony Orchestra at age 21. Five years later he went to the Cleveland Orchestra, then to Boston, and back to Cleveland. Finally, he returned to Chicago, where he remained for 13 years.

When former I.U. School of Music Dean Wilfred Bain asked Farkas to come to the University in 1960, he was more than ready after 37 years of performing.

This article is reprinted from the July 1982 *Indiana Daily Student*

Farkas began teaching long before he came to I.U. "The day that I joined the Chicago Symphony, the phone started ringing," he said. "You can't help it. The moment you get into a good symphony job you're asked to be a teacher."

Students of Farkas say that he has an excellent practical approach to the study of the horn. He can translate playing problems into physical difficulties that can be corrected.

"I'm getting quite good at particular problems, and I've seen more than my fair share of them," Farkas said.

Farkas is the inventor of a device to study a player's embouchure. The instrument is shaped like a horn mouthpiece, but is open so the lips can be seen. With this device he has photographed the embouchures of 40 of the world's greatest horn players, to help his students see what to do right.

"I have students in just about every orchestra in the country, and in Europe as well," Farkas said. "I know this business, I know how to get them into an orchestra."

In addition to his photographic study, Farkas has three other books in print. His book, *The Art of French Horn Playing* continues to sell more than 2,000 copies each year. Farkas is currently working on a book about auditioning which he hopes to complete next year.

Now that he is leaving I.U., travel will become more important. At the end of June he will give lectures and recitals in Greensboro, North Carolina, during the Eastern Music Festival. Then he will travel to West Texas State University.

In spite of all the traveling, Farkas plans to keep his home in Bloomington. "We've decided we won't leave Bloomington because we like it so much," he said. "I live out in the country, and alongside the house I have an old log cabin that was built in 1855. It's a nice studio for teaching."

Farkas considers teaching to be the most important aspect of his career, and plans to continue teaching privately. "We wonder what we leave to the world," he said. "Concerts are forgotten in a few weeks, and recordings become out-dated. But your students carry on what you have learned."

Philip Farkas Discography

Chicago Symphony, 1939-1941, with Frederick Stock, conductor. All recorded on 78 r.p.m. discs

Brahms, *Tragic Overture*, Columbia Set X-214, 4/26/41

Brahms, *Serenade No. 1 (Minuet only)*, Columbia C-12909D (in Set X-214), 4/26/41

Brahms, *Symphony No. 3*, Columbia Set M-443/Entre RL-3103, 11/23/40

Enesco, *Rumanian Rhapsody #1*, Columbia 11608-D/Set X-203, Entre RL-3022, 4/25/41

Glazunov, *Carnival Overture*, Columbia C-11771D/Entre RL-3022, 4/26/41

Glazunov, *Two Waltzes Op. 47/51 (D & F Major)*, Columbia Set X-232/Entre RL-3022, 4/26/41

Gliere, *Symphony No. 3 (Scherzo only)*, Columbia C-11697D, Entre RL-3022, 4/25/41

Ippolitov-Ivanov, *Procession of Sardar*, Columbia 11738-D, Entre RL-3022, 1/17/40

Mozart, *Symphony No. 38 in D "Prague"*, Columbia Set M-410, Entre RL-3026, 3/11 & 4/10/40

Paganini, *Moto Perpetuo (arr. Stock)*, Columbia 11738-D, 4/26/41

Ponchielli, *La Gioconda "Dance of the Hours"*, Columbia C-116221D/Entre RL-3022, 4/26/41

Reznicek, *Donna Diana Overture*, Columbia 11607-D/Set X-203, Entre RL-3002, 4/25/41

Saint-Saens, *Cello Concerto in A Minor (Piatigorsky)*, Columbia Set X-282, 3/6/40

Saint-Saens, *Danse Macabre*, Columbia C-11251D Entre RL-3022, 1/12/40

Schubert, *Symphony No. 9 in C Major*, Columbia Set M-403/Entre RL-3008, 1/12/40

Schumann, *Symphony No. 4*, Columbia Set M-475 Entre RL-3026, 4/25/41

Sibelius, *Swan of Tuonela*, Columbia 11388-D/Entre RL-3002, 4/10/40

Strauss, *Also Sprach Zarathustra*, Columbia Set M-421, 1/17/40

Tchaikovsky, *Violin Concerto (Milstein)*, Columbia M-413, ML-4053/Entre RL-3032/6631, 3/6/40

Tchaikovsky, *Nutcracker Suite*, Columbia Set M-395,
   Entre RL-3022,11/28/39
Toch, *Pinocchio, A Merry Overture*, Columbia C-11665D,
   DPL1-0490, 4/26/41
Walton, *Scapino Overture*, Columbia 11945-D/RCA DPL1-0245,
   4/26/41
Weber, *Euryanthe Overture*, Columbia 11179-D, 1/17/40

Cleveland Orchestra, 1941-1942, with A. Rodzinski, conductor.
All recorded on 78 r.p.m. discs
Debussy, *La Mer*, Columbia Set M-531
Jarnefelt, *Praeludium*, Columbia Set M-514
Kern, *Showboat Scenario*, Columbia Set M-495
Mendelssohn, *Midsummer Night's Dream*, Columbia Set M-504
Ravel, *Daphnis & Chloe, 2nd Suite*, Columbia Set X-230
Shostakovitch, *Symphony No. 5*, Columbia Set M-520
Sibelius, *Symphony No. 5*, Columbia Set M-514
Strauss, *Salome's Dance*, Columbia 11781-D
Weber, *Der Freischutz Overture*, Columbia 11817 D ·

Boston Symphony, 1945-1946, with S. Koussevitzky, conductor. All recorded on 78 r.p.m. discs
Copland, *Appalachian Spring*, RCA Victor
Copland, *Lincoln Portrait*, RCA Victor DM-1088
Prokofiev, *Romeo & Juliet Suite #2*, RCA Victor 11-9610-A
Prokofiev, *Symphony No. 5*, RCA Victor DM-1095

The Cleveland Orchestra, 1946-1947, with G. Szell, conductor.
Beethoven, *Symphony No. 4 (c. 1946)*

W.G.N. Orchestra, 1950

Humperdinck, *Hansel and Gretel excerpts*, Silvertone Records
   (Sears and Roebuck)
Tchaikovsky, *Symphony No. 2* (Broadcast)
Respighi, *Roman Festivals* (Broadcast)

Chicago Symphony, 1947-1951, with A. Rodzinski, conductor
Khatchaturian, *Gayne Ballet Suite No. 1*, RCA M-1212/Camden
   CFL-102, 11/18/47

Mendelssohn, *Symphony No. 3*, RCA M-1285/LM-1053, 11/18/47

Strauss, *Also Sprach Zarathustra*, RCA M-1285/LM-1060, 11/17/47

Wagner, *Tristan: Prelude to Act III*, RCA M-1258, 11/17/47

Wagner, *Prelude & Love Death*, RCA M-1230/V-21/LM-1060, 12/13/47

Chicago Symphony Orchestra, with R. Kubelik, conductor

Brahms, *Symphony No. 1*, Mercury 18023/14023/50007, 4/21/52

Dvorak, *New World Symphony*, Mercury MG 50002/18022/14022 MG3-4501, 11/20-21/51

Hindemith, *Symphonic Metamorphoses*, Mercury Classics MG 50024/50027/MG3-4501, 4/4/53

Mozart, *Symphony No. 34 & No. 38*, Mercury Classics MG 50015/14022/18022, #34: 12/6/52, #38: 4/3/53

Mussorgsky, *Pictures at an Exhibition*, Mercury 18028/14028/50000/ MG3-4500, 4/23-24/51

Schoenberg, *Five Pieces, Op. 16*, Mercury MG 50024/50026/75036, 4/4/53

Smetana, *Ma Vlast*, Mercury Classics DL-2-100/18026/14026, 12/4-6/52

Tchaikovsky, *Symphony No. 4*, Mercury MG 50003/14024/18024/ MG3-4501, 11/19-20/51

Tchaikovsky, *Symphony No. 6*, Mercury 18020/14020/50006, MG3-4500, 4/22/52

Chicago Symphony Orchestra, with A. Dorati, conductor

Bartok, *Miraculous Mandarin*, Mercury M-50038/50101, 1/29-30/54

Kodaly, *Peacock Variations*, Mercury M-50038, 1/29-30/54

Schubert, *Symphony No. 8*, Mercury 18018/14018/50037, 1/29-30/54

Tchaikovsky, *Romeo & Juliet Overture-Fantasy*, Mercury M-50037/14018/18018, 1/29-30/54

Chicago Symphony, 1954-1960, with Fritz Reiner, conductor

Albeniz, *Iberia, Fete-Dieu & Triana/Navarra*, LM-LSC-2230, CD RCD1-5404, 4/26/58

Bartok, *Concerto for Orchestra*, LM-LSC-1934/CD 5604-2-RC 10/22/55

Bartok, *Hungarian Sketches*, LM-LSC-2374, 12/29/58

Beethoven, *Coriolanus Overture*, LM-LSC-2343, 5/4/59

Beethoven, *Fidelio Overture, Op. 72*, LM-LSC-1991, 12/12/55

Beethoven, *Symphony No. 3, "Eroica"*, LM-1899, 12/4/54

Beethoven, *Symphony No. 5, Op. 67*, LM-LSC-2343,
    CD RCD1-5403, 5/4/59

Beethoven, *Symphony No. 7, Op. 92*, LM-LSC-1991,
    CD 6376-2-RC, 12/24/55

Borodin, *Prince Igor March*, LM-LSC-2423 (del.)/VICS-1068,
    3/14/59

Brahms, *Piano Concerto No. 1, (A. Rubenstein)*, LM-1831,
    CD 5668-2-RC, 4/17/54

Brahms, *Piano Concerto No. 2 (Emil Gilels)*, LM-LSC-2219(del.)
    VICS-1026/RCD1-5406, 2/8 & 10/58

Brahms, *Concerto for Violin & Orchestra (Heifetz)*, LM-LSC-1903,
    CD RCD1-5402, 2/21-22/55

Brahms, *Symphony No. 3, Op. 90*, LM-LSC-2209, 12/14/57

Brahms, *Tragic Overture*, LM-2209/LSC-2241, 12/14/57

Debussy, *Images: Iberia*, LSC-2222 (del.)/VICS-1025,
    CD RCD1-4934, 3/4/57

Debussy, *La Mer*, LM-LSC-2462/CD RCD1-7018, 2/27/60

DeFalla, *La Vida Breve & Three Cornered Hat*, LM-LSC-2230,
    CD RCD1-5404, 4/26/58

Dvorak, *Carnival Overture, Op. 92*, LM-1999/VICS-1424,
    CD5606-2-RC, 1/7/56

Dvorak, *New World Symphony, Op. 95*, LM-LSC-2214,
    CD-5606-2-RC, 11/9/57

Glinka, *Russlan & Ludmilla Overture*, LM-LSC-2423 (del.)
    VICS-1068m, 3/14/59

Granados, *Goyescas, Intermezzo*, LM-LSC-2230, 4/26/58

Haydn, *Symphony No. 88 in G Major*, LM-LSC-6087,
    VICS-1366, 2/26/60

Hovhannes, *Mysterious Mountain, Op. 132*, LM-LSC-2251,
    CD 5733-2-RC, 4/28/58

Kabalevsky, *Colas Breugnon Overture, Op. 24*, LM-LSC-2423
    (del.)/VICS-1068, 3/14/59

Liebermann, *Concerto for Jazz Band and Orchestra*, LM-1888,
    12/6/54

Liszt, *Mephisto Waltz*, LM-1999 (del.)/VICS-1025, 12/10/55

Liszt, *Todtentanz (B.Janis)*, LM-LSC-2541, 2/23/59

Mahler, *Das Lied von der Erde (Forrester, Lewis)*, LM-LSC-6087,
  VICS-1390/CD 5248-2-RC, 11/7 & 9/59
Mahler, *Symphony No. 4 (L. della Casa, sop.)*, LM-LSC-2364,
  CD 5722-2-RC, 4/26/55
Mendelssohn, *Fingal's Cave Overture, Op. 26*, LM-LSC-2241,
  VICS-1424, 1/7/56
Mozart, *Concerto for Piano & Orch. #25 in C*, LM-LSC-2287,
  2/15/58
Mozart, *Divertimento No. 17 in D, KV 337*, LM-1966,
  CD 6376-2-RC, 4/26/55
Mozart, *Don Giovanni Overture, KV 527*, LM-LSC-2287,
  3/14/59
Mozart, *Symphonies No. 36 & No. 41*, LM-6035/LM-2114,
  VICS-1336, 4/26/54
Mozart, *Symphony No. 39, KV 543*, LM-6035, 4/23/55
Mozart, *Symphony No. 40, KV 550*, LM-6035/LM-2114, 4/25/55
Mussorgsky, *Night on Bald Mountain*, LSC-2424 (del.)
  VICS-1068, CD 5602-2-RC, 3/14/59
Mussorgsky, *Pictures at an Exhibition (orch. Ravel)*, LM-LSC-2201
  CD RCS1-5407, 12/7/57
Prokofiev, *Alexander Nevsky Op. 78 (R. Elias)*, LM-LSC-2395/
  CD 5605-2-RC, 3/7 & 9/59
Prokofiev, *Lt. Kije Suite, Op. 60*, LM-LSC-2150/CD 5602-2-RC,
  3/2/57
Rachmaninoff, *Piano Concerto No. 1 (B. Janis)*, LM-2127 (del.)
  VICS-1101, 3/2/57
Rachmaninoff, *Piano Concerto No. 2 (Rubenstein)*, LM-LSC-2068,
  CD RCD1-4934, 1/9/56
Rachmaninoff, *Isle of the Dead, Op. 29*, LM-LSC-2183, 4/13/57
Rachmaninoff, *Rhapsody on a Theme of Paganini, Op. 43*,
  LM-LSC-2430/CD RCD1-4934, 1/16/56
Ravel, *Alborada del Gracioso*, LM-LSC-2222/VICS-1199,
  CD 5720-2-RC, 4/13/57
Ravel, *Pavanne for a Dead Princess*, LM-LSC-2183/VICS-1199,
  CD 5720-2-RC, 3/2/57
Ravel, *Rhapsodie Espagnole*, LM-LSC-2183/CD 5720-2-RC,
  11/3/56
Ravel, *Valses Nobles et Sentimentales*, LM-LSC-2222/VICS-1199,
  CD 5720-2-RC, 4/15/57
Respighi, *Pines & Fountains of Rome*, LM-LSC-2446,
  CD RCD1-5407, 10/24/59

Rimsky-Korsakov, *Scheherezade, Op. 25,* LM-LSC-2446,
CD RCD1-7018, 2/8/60
Rossini, *Overtures-Barber of Seville/Cenerentola/William Tell/
La Scala di Seta, Il Signor Bruschino,* LM-LSC-2318, 11/22/58
Schubert, *Symphony No. 5 in B Flat,* LM-LSC-2516, 4/27/60
Schubert, *Symphony No. 8 in B Minor,* LM-LSC-2516,
CD RCD1-5403, 3/26/60
Schumann, *Piano Concerto in A Minor (V. Cliburn),*
LM- LSC-2455, 4/16/60
Smetana, *Bartered Bride Overture,* LM-1999/VICS-1424,
12/12/55
J. Strauss, *Waltzes (various),* LM-LSC-2500/CD RCD1-5405,
4/25-26/60
J. Strauss, *Village Swallows Waltzes, Op. 164,* LM-LSC-2112,
CD RCD1-5405, 4/15/57
J. Strauss, Jr., *Waltzes (Blue Danube, Emperor, etc.),*
LM-LSC-2112/CD RCD1-5405, 4/15/57
Strauss, *Also Sprach Zarathustra, Op. 30,* LM-LSC-1806,
VICS-1265/CD 5721-2-RC, 3/18/54
Strauss, *Le Bourgeois Gentilhomme, Op. 60,* LM-6047,
VICS 1265/CD 5721-2-RC, 4/17-18/56
Strauss, *Burleske for Piano & Orchestra (B. Janis),* LM-2127 (del.)
VICS-1101/CD 5734-2-RC, 3/2/57
Strauss, *Don Juan, Op. 20,* LM-1888/VICS-1392,
CD RCD1-5408, 12/6/54
Strauss, *Don Juan, Op. 20,* LM-LSC-2462, 2/6/60
Strauss, *Don Quixote, Op. 35 (Janigro, Preves),* LD-LDS-2384,
CD 5734-2-RC, 4/11/59
Strauss, *Ein Heldenleben, Op. 40,* LM 1807 (del.)/VICS-1042,
CD RCD1-5408, 3/6/54
Strauss, *Elektra (selected scenes),* LM-6047/CD 5603-2-RC,
4/14-16/56
Strauss, *Rosenkavalier Waltzes (arr. Reiner),* LM-LSC-2112,
CD 5721-2-RC, 4/15/57
Strauss, *Salome, Op. 54 (Dance of the Seven Veils),* LM-1806,
VICS-1424, 3/6/54
Strauss, *Salome, Final Scene (Inge Borkh, sop.),* LM-6047,
VICS-1392/CD 5603-2-RC, 12/10/55
Strauss, *Sinfonia Domestica, Op. 53,* LM-2107/VICS-1104,
11/5/56

Stravinsky, *Fairy's Kiss, Divertimento,* LM-LSC-2251,
   CD 5733-2-RC4/28/58
Stravinsky, *Song of the Nightingale,* LM-LSC-2150,
   CD 5733-2-RC, 11/3/56
Tchaikovsky, *Marche Slave & Marche Miniature, Op. 43,*
   LSC-2423 (del.)/VICS-1068/CD 5602-2-RC, 3/14/59
Tchaikovsky, *Nutcracker Excerpts, Op. 71,* LM-LSC-2328,
   CD 5642-2-RC, 3/21/59
Tchaikovsky, *Piano Concerto No. 1 (E. Gilels),* LM-1969 (del.)
   VICS-1039, 10/29/55
Tchaikovsky, *Violin Concerto (Heifetz),* LM-LSC-2129, 4/18/57
Tchaikovsky, *1812 Overture, Op. 49,* LM-1999 (del.)
   VICS-1025/CD 5642-2-RC, 1/7/56
Tchaikovsky, *Symphony No. 6, Op. 74 (Pathetique),* LM-LSC-
   2216/CD 5602-2-RC, 4/16/57
Wagner, *Die Meistersinger excerpts,* LM-LSC-2441,
   CD RCD1-4738, 4/18/59
Wagner, *Siegfried's Rhine Journey & Funeral Music,* LM-LSC-
   2441/CD RCD1-4738, 4/18/59
Weber, *Invitation to the Dance, Op. 65,* LM-LSC-2112, 4/15/57
Weinberger, *Schwanda Polka & Fugue,* LM-1999/VICS-1424,
   CD 5606-2-RC, 1/7/56

Chicago Symphony Orchestra, with W. Hendl, conductor
Beethoven, *Piano Concerto No. 3 (Graffman),* LM-LSC-2396,
   VICS-1059, 5/5/59
Lalo, *Symphonie Espagnole (Szeryng),* LM-LSC-2456/VICS-1064,
   2/28/59
Sibelius, *Violin Concerto (Heifetz),* LM-LSC-2435/4010,
   1/10&12/59

Solo and Chamber Music
American Woodwind Quintet
"Contemporary American Music" Golden Crest records CR
   4075 (c. 1970)

Benson, Warren, *Marche*
Bright, Houston, *Short Dances*
Haddad, Donald, *Blues au Vent*
Kaufmann, Walter, *Partita*
White, Donald, *Three for Five*
Zaninelli, Luigi, *Dance Variations*

American Woodwind Quintet
Coronet 1709
Heiden, Bernard, *Intrada (woodwind and sax)*

Chicago Symphony Woodwind Quintet — Woodwind Quintets
Audiophile Records AP-14, AP-15, AP-16, AP-17
Chaminade, Cecil, *Scarf Dance* (17)
Danzi, *Quintet, Op. 56, No. 2* (16)
Debussy, *Golliwog's Cakewalk* (17, Saga 5361)
Debussy, *The Little Negro* (14)
Delibes, *La Source* (17)
Dvorak, *Humoresque, Op. 101/7* (17)
Gould, Morton, *Pavanne* (17)
Guentzel, Gus, *Scherzo, Op. 17* (16)
Guion, David, *The Harmonica Player* (17)
Hartley, G., *Divertissement* (16)
Haydn, *Capriccio* (17)
Haydn, *Presto,* (16)
Hindemith, *Kleine Kammermusik, Op. 24/2* (15)
Huffer, Fred, *Sailor's Hornpipe* (17)
Hunter, Eugene, *Danse Humoresque* (17)
Ibert, *Three Short Pieces* (15)
Klughardt, August, *Quintet Op. 79* (14)
Leclair, Jean-Marie, *Minuet & Hunting Scene* (14)
Lefebvre, Charles, *Suite Op. 57* (16)
Milhaud, D., *La Cheminee du Roi Rene,* (15)
Mussorgsky, *Ballet of Chicks in Shells,* (17)
Mozart, *Menuet* (17)
Paganini, *La Chasse* (16)
Pierne, *Entrance of the Little Fauns* (17)
Pierne, *March of the Tin Soldiers* (17, Saga-5361)
Pietsch, *Lullaby & Humoresque* (17)
Ravel, *Piece en forme de Habanera* (16)
Rimsky-Korsakov, *Flight of the Bumblebee* (16)
Shostakovitch, *Polka* (14)
Somis, G., *Adagio & Allegro from Violin Sonata* (16)
Stravinsky, *Pastorale* (14)
Tchaikovsky, *Humoresque* (17)

Philip Farkas French Horn Solos (with pianist Marion Hall)
Coronet Recording Stereo #1293-S

Bozza, Eugene, *En Foret, Op. 40*
Francaix, *Canon in Octave*
Gallay, *Unmeasured Preludes*
Glazunov, A., *Reverie in D flat, Op. 24*
Gliere, R., *Intermezzo, Op. 35*
Piantoni, L., *Air de Chasse*
Schumann, R., *Adagio & Allegro, Op. 70 in A flat*

Dick Shory Percussion (3 albums):

"Wild Percussion and Horns A' Plenty", RCA Victor LSP2289 (with Ethel Merker & Frank Brouk)

"Runnin' Wild", RCA Victor LSA2306

"World of Alcina/Bill Russo" on Atlantic 1241 Records (Phil Farkas & Frank Brouk, horns)

Recording with Nat King Cole, *"Portrait of Jenny"*

Jingles with Budweiser Beer and United Airlines

Getting a new mouthpiece the hard way

156

EPILOGUE

Readers of this book are undoubtedly convinced of the unique qualities of Philip Farkas; the productivity of this man far surpasses that of any other brass performer and would rival any individual in the music business. Phil carries this off with the relaxed, friendly attitude of a confident person at home with the world.

Then there is that grand lady, Peggy! The old adage, "Behind every great man," etc., etc., has some application in this case. Those who know the Farkas family will agree that Phil has had a terrific wife standing beside him all the way. Peggy is at once unassuming and strong, proud and humble, regal and homey. Her support and encouragement have been very important in the development of the Farkas legacy, yet she is quick to put the accolades in the proper perspective and get on with the important details of life. Peggy and Phil have great pride in their family and Peggy has supplied the continuity and persistence to make it all work.

Each contributor in this study has approached the subject from a different perspective. The picture of Phil Farkas gradually emerges and the extent of his successful talents become evident. My personal association with Phil has been unique and stimulating; although we have had many areas of contact over the years, the most meaningful have been the times that I joined Phil and Mike Hatfield for their Tuesday lunches at Bear's Place, across the street from the I.U. School of Music. One cannot help feeling the great enthusiasm and joy of this man; stories, anecdotes, humor, etc. are often initiated even before the waitress arrives and could continue long past dessert. Frequently, one returns to the studio exhausted from laughter and the effort of trying to keep up with Phil, but always with the renewed exhilaration of great music and the desire to communicate this excitement to students and audiences. It is hoped that some of Philip Farkas' contagious spirit comes through the pages of this book.

M. Dee Stewart